CURIOUS
EDINBURGH

MICHAEL T.R.B. TURNBULL

SUTTON PUBLISHING

First published in the United Kingdom in 2005 by
Sutton Publishing Limited · Phoenix Mill
Thrupp · Stroud · Gloucestershire · GL5 2BU

Reprinted 2006 (twice)

British Library Cataloguing in Publication Data
A catalogue record for this book is available from the British Library.

ISBN 0-7509-3949-4

Title page photograph: detail from *Manuscript of Monte Cassino,* by Eduardo Paolozzi

To Dillon

Typeset in Janson 10.5/13.5pt.
Typesetting and origination by
Sutton Publishing Limited.
Printed and bound in England by
J.H. Haynes & Co. Ltd, Sparkford.

CONTENTS

Acknowledgements and Picture Credits   4

Introduction   5

Old Town   7

Edinburgh Castle   9

Castle Esplanade   14

The Royal Mile   20

Castlehill   24

Cowgate   30

Lawnmarket   32

High Street   41

Canongate   70

Holyroodhouse   81

Southside   89

New Town   95

First New Town   95

Eastern New Town   107

Western New Town   117

Northern New Town   123

Outer Edinburgh   129

Outer Edinburgh (South)   129

Outer Edinburgh (North)   136

Outer Edinburgh (East)   142

Outer Edinburgh (West)   150

Discovering Edinburgh's Past   153

Other Useful Contact Details   156

Further Reading   160

ACKNOWLEDGEMENTS AND PICTURE CREDITS

To my grandparents who first brought me to Edinburgh and my late Aunt Barbara who introduced me to its magic. I also acknowledge a debt to Dr W. J. Macpherson of Gonville and Caius College, Cambridge, who first awakened in me an abiding interest in local history.

Thanks are due to the following organisations that have kindly given permission for illustrations to be published:

City of Edinburgh Council (53, 55, 78 (2), 91, 101, 102, 140); Cockburns (151); Dean Cemetery Trust (106); Edinburgh Military Tattoo (19); Edinburgh University (40, 75, 92); George Heriot's School (89); Historic Scotland (4, 11, 12, 13, 15, 16, 17, 19, 135, 142); Joe Hagan (26); Napier University (131); National Trust for Scotland (145); Prestonfield (144); Real Mary King's Close (54); Royal Botanic Garden (126, 127); Royal Commission on the Ancient and Historic Monuments of Scotland (RCAHMS) (5, 9, 31, 62, 74 [Chrystal Collection]); St Giles Cathedral (47).

Francis Caird Inglis (10, 12, 32, 44, 45, 69, 76, 82, 96, 104, 141). Every effort has been made to locate the copyright holder of the photographs from F.C. Inglis' *Dear Auld Reekie* (Edinburgh: Homeland Association, 1925) and permission will be requested when such is located.

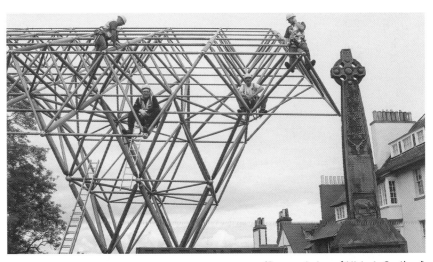

(By permission of Historic Scotland)

INTRODUCTION

Edinburgh Old and New

Curiosity is part of the human condition. The title *Curious Edinburgh* reflects the city's long history of scientific and philosophical enquiry – from Sir Arthur Conan Doyle (who, while a medical student, based his celebrated investigator partly on his observations of the work of Dr Joseph Bell, a surgeon at the Edinburgh Infirmary), to the unsettling philosophical investigations of David Hume, to generations of the Darwin family who came to Edinburgh to study medicine (including, however briefly, Charles Darwin, author of *The Origin of Species*), to James Clerk Maxwell and his epoch-defining revelation that light was an electromagnetic phenomenon.

Moreover, with royal heralds proclaiming the death of kings at the Mercat Cross, with the ubiquitous eighteenth-century cadies (messengers), with 'Flying Stationers' distributing sensational broadside texts in the street, the residents of Edinburgh have revelled in gossip,

news and information: newspapers and the publishing industry helped make Edinburgh a city where curiosity was a way of life.

But there is another side to curiosity. Edinburgh, as it spread ever wider, consuming the villages around it, also rejoiced in eccentricity: bizarre characters, such as Lord Henry Cockburn lovingly described in his *Memorials of His Time* (1856) or the barber turned etcher John Kay (1742–1826) wickedly satirised in acerbic caricature; a walk down the Royal Mile soon uncovers rare and unusual facts or arcane architectural flourishes, while a visit to one of the city's historic graveyards opens the door to a beguiling theatre of death.

*   *   *   *

Curious Edinburgh also hints at the darker side of the city. Edinburgh, for all its diversity crammed into so small a space, quickly makes the prudent observer aware of the deeper tensions underlying the capital's urbane exterior.

Such fractures penetrate the very landscape – the topography of Old Town and New, for example. The former grew slowly and organically, interacting with the awkwardness of its volcanic foundation; the bewildering complexity of its architecture and the rigid stratification of its towering lands (tenements) encouraged what has been aptly called 'the democracy of the common stair', where bourgeois and beggar were regularly forced to engage with each other as they climbed up – or stepped down. The design of the New Town, by contrast, was rigidly geometric, mechanically conceived; imposed on the landscape, it was designed to cultivate social exclusion and stratification.

At the core of the city lies Edinburgh's divided heart: on the one hand, the reviled and stony Heart of Midlothian, hated symbol of official brutality; on the other, the graceful Luckenbooth Brooch, with inter-twined hearts and the memory of the beautiful but doomed Mary, Queen of Scots.

Literary Edinburgh still resonates with Robert Louis Stevenson's chilling portrayal of the dual personalities of Dr Jekyll and Mr Hyde, partly based as they were on the 'devious Deacon', William Brodie. A powerful study of repression and the subconscious, this novel anticipated the published work of Sigmund Freud by some ten years.

Politically, Edinburgh in 1603 was especially wounded and culturally impoverished by the departure to London of James VI of Scotland. It took him fourteen long years to return to the city (this time as James I), having left Edinburgh's institutions and ceremonial buildings increasingly bereft of power and dignity, a condition to which the Union of the Parliaments (1707) set the seal. Today a new Scottish parliament, controversial as its price and design may be, will go some way to enhance Edinburgh's capital status.

OLD TOWN

'You are caves of guilt, you are pinnacles of jubilation' wrote the poet Norman MacCaig (1910–96) of his home town and its many contrasts and ironies. As MacCaig knew only too well, Edinburgh (like any great city) is a marriage of ancient and modern, of vice and virtue. First, the gloomy, dark and fossilised Old Town growing organically in eccentric spirals and gravity-defying tenements gripping the volcanic rock and its sloping crag-and-tail; then the eighteenth-century gleaming New Town rises to the north, symmetrical and deliberately rectangular but for its elegantly circular places and crescents; then the later absorptions of the village communities which surrounded the metropolis.

The Old Town grew out of two quite separate burghs (towns licensed to trade): Edinburgh and Canongate. First came a fortified settlement high on what would be the Castlehill; later, the Canongate was set up as the domain of the Augustinian canons living at the foot of the slope in the Abbey of Holyrood – military force counterbalanced by religious power (gunpowder and incense). In the eighteenth century the organic complexity, overcrowding and disorder of the Old Town was overtaken by the cool regularity of the New Town: the physical contact and mysterious enticements of the medieval rabbit-warren were replaced by Robert Louis Stevenson's 'windy parallelograms', the wide open spaces (where neighbours could so easily pretend not to notice each other) encouraged by the emotional detachment and logical philosophies of the Age of Reason. In the nineteenth and twentieth centuries came the encroachment of the city on to the intimate villages of outer Edinburgh and, finally, the tearing out of the heart of the city as whole communities were decanted into peripheral housing schemes.

Today the Royal Mile stretches from Edinburgh Castle to the Palace of Holyroodhouse; it encloses at its summit the medieval walled town of Edinburgh (running from the Castle to the Netherbow Port, with Castle, Castlehill, Lawnmarket and High Street). At the Netherbow Port (with its World's End pub) was the southern main gate out of Edinburgh, marking the beginning of the second burgh – the Canongate (canons' gait), the preserve of the Augustinian canons of Holyrood Abbey.

Stony-hearted

Over the centuries Edinburgh has inspired delight but also revulsion from visitors struck by the two contrasting faces of the Old Town. 'Stony-hearted Edinburgh!' complained the literary critic William Hazlitt in 1822, 'What art thou to me? The dust of thy streets mingles with my tears and blinds me. City of palaces, or of tombs – a quarry, rather than the habitation of men!' The adventurer R.B. Cunninghame Graham (1934) observed that 'Edinburgh has become a mere shell of itself, a mere empty tabernacle, a city without a soul', while in the following year the novelist and poet Edwin Muir added scathingly that 'Edinburgh presents outwardly the face it had a hundred years ago, while within it is worm-eaten with all the ingenuity in tastelessness which modern resources can supply'.

Others were genuinely astonished at the scale of a city which conjured up a scene from Jonathan Swift's *Gulliver's Travels*: 'What a wonderful City Edinburgh is! – What alteration of Height and Depth! – a city looked at in the polish'd back of a Brobdignag Spoon, held lengthways – so enormously stretched-up are the Houses!' marvelled the poet Samuel Taylor Coleridge (1803), while G.K. Chesterton (1905) enthused that 'Great buildings rush up like rockets'.

EDINBURGH CASTLE

'The Castle Rock of Edinburgh is, as far as I know,' wrote English art historian and critic John Ruskin, in 1857, 'simply the noblest in Scotland conveniently unapproachable by any creatures but sea-gulls or peewits.' Not only is Edinburgh Castle today the most-visited paying visitor attraction in Scotland, but excavations in 1988–91 revealed ancient hilltop settlements on the Castle Rock which date from the late Bronze Age and make the castle the longest continuously occupied site in Scotland. Being a place of relative safety, the castle was used to store a variety of precious objects. David I, for example, lodged his 'Black Kist' (chest) there. The kist contained, among other items, the *sark* (shirt) of Robert the Bruce. James III kept his 'Black Rood' (cross) in the castle. This relic of the True Cross of Christ was in his hands when he died at the castle in 1153. Most famous of all, however, are the 'Honours of Scotland', the regalia of the Scottish monarchy – the crown, sceptre and the sword of state.

The crown dates from 1540, when fresh gold was added to a circlet of Robert I. It is made up of 4 pounds of Scottish gold and contains 22 semi-precious stones from the Scottish mountains and 96 mussel pearls, mainly from the River Tay. The sceptre was given to James IV in 1494 by Pope Alexander VI, while the sword of state was the gift of Pope Julius II (1507). In the same room are James VI's Order of the Garter and the chains of the Order of the Thistle belonging to James VII. Today they have been joined by the historic Stone of Scone (the Stone of

Access

Entry to the Castle Esplanade is free of charge but there is a parking fee for cars (otherwise park to the south or north of the castle). Take care to explain to the attendants at the entry cabin what you are planning to do and they will almost always be sympathetic and helpful. Access to the castle itself is paid. Again, ask for help and guidance either when buying a ticket or when showing it at the drawbridge.

The castle is managed by Historic Scotland. When armed sentries are on duty either at the foot of the esplanade or in the sentry-boxes photographs may be taken, but ask a member of Historic Scotland staff just in case.

(Crown copyright: RCAHMS)

(Copyright: F.C. Inglis)

Destiny) on which the ancient kings of Scotland were crowned. Used for the coronation of Charles I and Charles II, the Honours were later hidden in Kineff Church near Aberdeen before being deposited in the Crown Room at the Castle where their existence was forgotten for almost a hundred years. In 1817 they were rediscovered, largely through the persistence of Sir Walter Scott, and were used to good effect during George IV's state visit to Scotland in 1822. At various times the castle also contained the Scottish Archives and the Scottish Mint. Today Edinburgh Castle provides a magnificent setting for the annual Edinburgh Military Tattoo – in 2004 the second most popular of all the events during the Edinburgh International Festival, with an income of £23.3m.

St Margaret's Chapel

Access

On the highest point of the Castle Rock, reached either by the steep Lang Stairs or the more leisurely approach by Foog's Gate.

As a boy the novelist George Borrow (1803–81) spent some time in Edinburgh and never forgot the softer side of the castle and its rock (whose steep slope he enjoyed clambering over): 'I soon found that the rock contained all manner of strange crypts, crannies and recesses, where owls nestled and the weasel brought forth her young.' All that remains of Edinburgh's ancient fortress (once known as the Castle of the Maidens) is a narrow rectangular chapel built in about AD 1110 in the name of Queen Margaret of Scotland (*c.* 1046–93), saintly wife of King Malcolm Canmore. Born in Hungary in about AD 1046, Margaret died in 1093 three days after she had been given news of the deaths of her husband and her eldest son in battle at Alnwick in Northumberland. It was Margaret's youngest son, King David (1124–53), who was determined that Scotland should share in the benefits which monasteries had already brought to France and England. He arranged for monks from a number of religious orders to come to Scotland and encouraged them in the construction of their monasteries. During the reign of David II (1329–71) Edinburgh increased in size, and so did the importance of the castle.

(By permission of Historic Scotland)

The Great Hall

Access

On the southern side of Crown Square.

One of the earliest descriptions of eating in Edinburgh comes from the sixth-century poet Aneurin. Writing in the Brythonic language, he records the deeds of the Gododdin, a Celtic tribe known to the Romans as the Votadini. Aneurin tells how in about AD 590 King Mynyddog entertained an army of warriors in the great hall of the fort of Eidyn (Edinburgh), standing on what is now known as Castle Hill. Watched by the royal steward the warriors reclined on cushions and couches of white fleece, drinking from horns before the pine-logs burning in the great fire. Tapers lighting the hall glinted on gold and silver cups and glass tumblers filled with mead. They were preparing to ride south to battle at Catterick – sadly, to defeat and annihilation.

But food had a peaceful as well as a military function. According to her confessor and biographer Turgot, Queen Margaret of Scotland encouraged many civilising customs in Edinburgh at the otherwise rough and ready court of Malcolm Canmore. Among these was her habit of having nine orphan and destitute children brought to her early in the morning. She delighted in sitting them on her knee and, using her own silver spoons, feeding them with soft and nourishing food.

(Copyright: F.C. Inglis)

Food could also be a form of aggression. The most famous fifteenth-century meal at the castle (the 'Black Dinner' of November 1440) was an act of extreme savagery. Eighteen-year-old William, Earl of Douglas, and his young brother David were invited to dinner at the castle by King James II. During the dinner a bull's head was carried to the table: this was the signal for the earl and his brother to be seized (in spite of the protests and tears of the king), taken to the Castlehill and immediately executed for treason. The injustice and cruelty of the Black Dinner were condemned in an old ballad:

(By permission of Historic Scotland)

> Edinburgh Castle, toune and toure,
> God grant thou sink for sinne!
> And that even for the black dinoir
> Earl Douglas got therein.

The castle was not all inhumanity to man, however. There were more civilising aspects such as the cuisine: the royal cooks grew fancy ingredients in the castle gardens to tease the jaded royal palate – violets were served as a salad herb, eaten raw with onions and lettuce; roses and primroses were cooked with milk, sugar or honey – each a 'dainty dish to set before a king'. From Scotland's Exchequer Rolls emerge intriguing details of the kings' shopping-basket. The gourmands in the Scottish royal household delighted in aromatic and dried fruits shipped from Alexandria and Damascus by Venetian and Genoese traders. In 1473 the cargoes included green ginger, cloves, mace, nutmeg, saffron, almonds, figs, raisins, dates, liquorice, pepper, caraway and cumin, many of which were used for softening the harsh taste of acidic wines. Royal feasts were often exotic: on Christmas Day 1511 King James IV entertained the French ambassador with jellies made from the feet of 500 oxen, 1,500 sheep and 36 cockerels. Minstrels serenaded the guests as they dined on swans and cranes.

Mons Meg

> Hark, when its sulph'rous vollies fly,
> How groans the earth! How roars the sky!

Access

On the north-facing ramparts of Edinburgh Castle.

So exclaimed Robert Alves, an astonished visitor to Edinburgh in 1789. The castle contained many cannon, but none more famous than the huge medieval bombard Mons Meg. Made for King James II in 1455, it was constructed at Mons in Flanders. In 1558 the cannon was fired during the marriage of Mary Stuart to the Dauphin of France and the cannon-ball was found 2 miles away. A report of 1734 describes Mons Meg's fearsome firepower: the bombard itself weighed 5.94 tons; its iron cannon-balls weighed 1,125 pounds, its stone ones 549 pounds; and some 105 pounds of powder were needed to fire it. With an elevation of 45 degrees, Mons Meg was able to fire an iron ball 1,408 yards and a stone one 2,867 yards, in 16 and 22 seconds respectively.

Mons Meg is sometimes confused with the cannon fired in celebration after the successful siege of Roxburgh Castle (held by the English) in 1460. The cannon exploded and King James II of Scotland, who was standing nearby, was injured in the leg by a flying wooden wedge. He later bled to death. Mons Meg did indeed burst, but this was in 1682, while firing a salute for King James VII (formerly enormously popular in Edinburgh as the Duke of York). In 1754 the cannon was removed to London but, through the influence of Sir Walter Scott, returned to Edinburgh in 1829. Today Mons Meg is located high on the ramparts of the castle, facing the New Town, the River Forth and the hills beyond.

(By permission of Historic Scotland)

CASTLE ESPLANADE

Sasine of Nova Scotia

The *sasine* (Scots legal term for 'possession') of Nova Scotia is a good example of legal fiction put to cunning political effect. The rank of baronet had originally been introduced by the cash-strapped King James VI and I as a way of raising money and colonising the provinces of Ulster by appealing to his subjects' hunger for promotion. Charles I revived the custom in order to persuade settlers to emigrate to Nova Scotia, a territory which had been granted to Sir William Alexander of Menstrie, Earl of Stirling. The number of baronetcies was limited to 150, each new baronet paying £3,000 for the privilege. To overcome the difficulty of giving rights of possession to a land overseas, the earth and stones of the Castlehill were converted by royal mandate into that of Nova Scotia and the new baronets given the rights of castle, pit and gallows in a ceremony supervised by the Lord Lyon and his heralds. The first new baronet was Sir Robert Gordon of Gordonstoun, Morayshire, created baronet on 26 May 1625. Between that date and 1649 some sixty-four baronets took *sasine* of their Nova Scotia territory, many staying at home and paying substitutes to do the hard work of colonisation. The tradition was commemorated in modern times when in January 1943 the Court of the Lord Lyon sent a sack of earth and stone from the castle and a beam of oak to be incorporated into the Tercentenary Monument at Annapolis, Nova Scotia. In October 1953 the Premier of Nova Scotia, the Rt Hon Angus Macdonald, unveiled a plaque on the Castle Esplanade commemorating the first baronets who received *sasine* of their 16,000-acre estate, and deposited a handful of earth from Nova Scotia into the dry moat of the castle.

72nd Duke of Albany's Own Highlanders Monument

A red granite obelisk erected by the regiment commemorates men killed in action or who died of wounds or disease during the 1878–80 campaign in Afghanistan. The Peterhead granite monument was the work of McDonald, Field & Company (1882–3). The regiment was originally raised in 1778 as the Earl of Seaforth's Regiment. In 1823 (having been deprived of the kilt after the Battle of Culloden) the regiment was again made a Highland one and in the following year, after an absence of twenty-four years, it returned to Scotland and was quartered at the castle. Recruitment for the 72nd began in the Highlands and a new uniform was designed, with Royal Stuart trews, red coatees and feather bonnets. On 1 August 1825 new colours were presented to the regiment at Edinburgh's Bruntsfield Links, together with a new regimental badge, comprising the cipher 'F' and the coronet of Prince Frederick, Duke of York. The Afghan campaign of 1877 was made necessary because the Afghans had allowed a Russian embassy to be opened but refused to accept a British

Mission in Kabul. The British government decided that a mission had to be established, by force if necessary. In November 1877 Major-General Frederick Roberts VC led his men into Afghanistan but was met by a hostile force at Peiwar Kotal Pass. On 2 December the right wing, composed of the 72nd Highlanders and the 5th Gurkhas, stormed the flank by night and captured twenty-one enemy guns. A severe winter was followed in May by the Treaty of Gandamach, by which the Afghans finally accepted the setting up of a British Mission. However, six weeks later the staff of the mission were massacred. General Roberts was ordered to occupy Kabul. An Afghan army some 12,000 strong blocked the passage of the British army in October; again the 72nd and the Gurkhas made a flank attack. At Charasiah the regiment carried its colours into battle for the last time. On 13 October General Roberts entered Kabul with 200 captured guns and 7,000 enemy

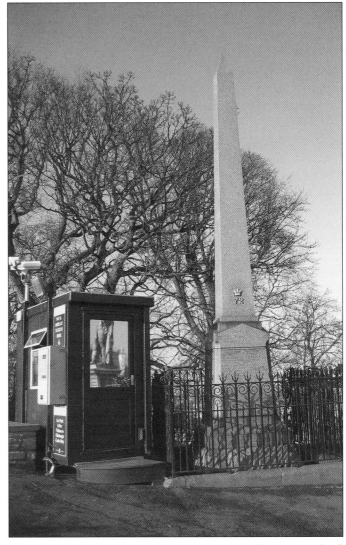

(By permission of Historic Scotland)

rifles, marching through the city to the music of military bands. In December 1879 the 72nd were encamped outside Kabul when a *Jihad* (holy war) was declared. The regiment was then active in the hills around the city. On 14 December, during fierce fighting, Lance-Corporal George Sellar had gone ahead armed with rifle and bayonet; in hand-to-hand combat he was severely wounded by an Afghan wielding a knife. General Roberts had watched the incident through his binoculars and Lance-Corporal Sellar was later awarded the Victoria Cross for bravery. In 1880 a 300-mile march was ordered; the temperature rose to 110 degrees Fahrenheit at midday and fell to freezing at midnight. For twenty-two days the army marched with no losses among the 10,000 troops. On 1 September they attacked the Afghan army at Kandahar; the 72nd were part of the left flank. In the battle two officers of the regiment (including the commander) and eleven men were killed.

Access

North-west side of
Castle Esplanade.

Ensign Ewart Monument

A Norwegian granite monument commemorates Ensign Charles Ewart of the North British Dragoons, who captured the eagle standard of the French 45th Regiment at Waterloo (from which the eagle badge worn by the Royal Scots Greys was derived). Ewart described the capture: 'A soldier thrust for my groin but I parried it off and cut him through to the head, after which I was attacked by one of their lancers, who threw his lance at me but missed the mark by my throwing it off with my sword. Then I cut him from chin upwards, which went through his teeth. Next I was attacked by a foot soldier who, after firing at me, charged me with his bayonet. But he very soon lost the combat, for I parried it and cut him down through the head. So that finished the contest for the eagle.' Ewart died in 1846 aged 77 years.

Access

North-west side of the
Castle Esplanade.

Duke of York Statue

With his back to Princes Street Gardens, Frederick, Duke of York and Albany (1763–1827), poses magnificently on the esplanade, dressed in the robes of a Knight of the Garter and holding a field marshal's baton as Commander of the British Army, in a bronze statue said to have been sculpted by John Greenshields (*c.* 1792–1838). The son of a small farmer on a Lanarkshire estate belonging to the brother of John Gibson

Lockhart (1794–1854), son-in-law and biographer of Sir Walter Scott, Greenshields was a stonemason by trade but aspired to become a sculptor. His statue of Scott in Parliament Hall is said to be a very good likeness. His bronze statue of the Duke of York was made for an exhibition in Edinburgh and erected on the esplanade in 1836, standing, as the children's song about the 'Grand Old Duke of York' says, 'at the top of the hill'. The statue is also attributed by architectural historians to Thomas Campbell (1839).

As Commander-in-Chief of the British army during the campaign of 1793 against the revolutionary French in Flanders, the duke began well, capturing Valenciennes and even being acclaimed King of France, but a series of tactical blunders led to his recall in December 1794 and the evacuation

(By permission of Historic Scotland)

from Dunkirk. In 1799 he was again Commander of the British army in Holland when his men were joined by 10,000 Russians who advanced too eagerly, causing an unexpected engagement on unfamiliar ground. The result was a humiliating negotiation and withdrawal. Such events produced popular derision (as in 'The Grand Old Duke of York') and even Wellington (then a young soldier) confessed years later that 'I learnt what one ought not to do, and that is always something!' Off the field of battle, the Duke of York was an able and successful administrator, building up the British army into an effective force that would later enable Wellington to defeat Napoleon.

(By permission of Historic Scotland)

Earl Haig Monument

Field-Marshal Earl Haig (1861–1928), Commander of the British forces during the First World War, looks keenly ahead on his horse. Haig's bronze statue was cast by G.F. Wade (see also New Town, 24 Charlotte Square, for a fuller account of his life, and the Museum of Edinburgh which displays a re-creation of Haig's First World War field headquarters along with other military equipment).

Access

North side of the Castle Esplanade.

Sundial

High on the wall of the Ramsay Lodge is a rust-coloured sundial gripped by a cherub. It forms part of a decorative window lintel and bears the date 1892. Around it is a quotation from the Greek dramatist Aeschylus (*c.* 525–456 BC), taken from his play *The Eumenides* (line 286) which tells how Orestes, son of King Agamemnon, horribly avenges the murder of his father by his mother, by killing her. He is then pursued by the savage Furies (barbaric witchlike creatures who bring death and punishment). Orestes defends himself by saying that 'Time cleanses all things in ageing them' (the quotation used by Sir Patrick Geddes on the wall of Ramsay Garden, his 'seven-towered castle built for his beloved'). The quotation below (in English) is from Robert Burns' 'A Man's a Man for a' that.'

Access

North-east side of the Castle Esplanade on the wall of Ramsay Lodge.

Access

On the east wall of the
Castle Esplanade.

The Witches' Fountain

Designed by John Duncan for Sir Patrick Geddes in 1894 and erected in 1912, this stylish bronze drinking fountain commemorates the 300 supposed witches who were tied at the stake, strangled and then burnt to ashes on the Castlehill between 1492 and 1722. The purpose of the drinking fountain is to record the fact that not all witches worked for evil. The serene head is Hygeia, goddess of health, and the serpent is the symbol of Aesculapius, god of medicine (still honoured by doctors today). Though the foxglove produces poisonous digitalis, it is also a thing of beauty, and the 'evil eye' can be kept at bay by the hands of healing. Through the cleansing fire on the centre panel passed black magicians and also the well-intentioned practitioners of homeopathic medicine, as well as elderly or bewildered persons wrongly deemed malevolent. King James VI and I (who was born at Edinburgh Castle) fuelled the popular paranoia about witches with his book *Dæmonologie* (1597). Seven years earlier the king suspected that witches had conjured up violent storms while he was sailing back to Scotland from Denmark. In the witch trial that

followed, men and women confessed under torture that 200 witches had sailed in sieves from Leith to North Berwick and then danced round the churchyard in the presence of the Devil. One woman claimed she had hung a black toad upside down for three days and then collected the venom in an oyster shell. The unfortunate suspects were deprived of sleep, tormented with thumb-screws and their legs crushed in the 'buits' (wooden wedges). Janet Horne, burnt at the stake in 1722, was the last witch to be executed in Scotland – although the persecution of so-called witches lasted for another thirty years in mainland Europe. In all, it is thought that over 4,500 'witches' were killed in Scotland.

Cannonball House

Cannonball House is so called from the two rusted iron balls (one now fragmented) which can be seen protruding from its wall. Two theories exist to explain the balls. In the first, they were cannonballs fired from the Castle's Half-Moon Battery in 1745 during the Jacobite siege. However, it is extremely unlikely that two cannonballs could embed themselves in a wall in such a neat straight line. The more likely explanation is that the iron balls are markers inserted in 1681 by the German engineer Peter Brusche, who was paid £3,000 to lay a 3-inch lead pipe from Comiston Springs Water House with its five springs – the Hare, the Fox, the Swan, the Lapwing and the Owl. (Some of these ornamental well-heads can be viewed at the Museum of Edinburgh in the Canongate.) The cannonballs probably mark the water-level of the distant springs. Opposite Cannonball House is the Castlehill Reservoir, first constructed in 1681 and replaced in 1851. It had a capacity of almost two million gallons, and was supplied by the Swanston and Alnwickhill reservoirs to the south of the city. The Reservoir (now the Edinburgh Old Town Weaving Company) once fed ten town wells, two of which can still be seen in the High Street off Parliament Square and outside John Knox's House.

Access

On the east side of the Esplanade, above the entry cabin.

Edinburgh Military Tattoo

Every August cleverly constructed scaffolding transforms the Castle Esplanade into an exciting amphitheatre for the Tattoo. The name is derived from 'Doe den tap toe', meaning 'Turn off the taps', which was the tavern closing-time call in the Low Countries. The first Tattoo was held by the Army in Scotland in 1950, and since then more than eleven million people have attended. The annual audience is about 217,000, with a hundred million watching on television, some 70 per cent of them outside Scotland. The Tattoo, with its stirring musical, dramatic and marching spectacles, has raised some £5 million for service and charitable organisations and has contributed £88 million to the Scottish economy.

Visit 'The Spirit of the Tattoo', 555 Castlehill. Tel: 0131 225 9661.

(By permission of Edinburgh Military Tattoo)

THE ROYAL MILE

Ramsay Garden

Access

A private residential complex just at the north-east end of the esplanade, to be admired but not disturbed.

Behind the former Castlehill Reservoir is fragrant and calm Ramsay Garden, built mainly by Patrick Geddes (1854–1932), the 'father of town planning', for his wife. It was constructed around the octagonal turret of Allan Ramsay's villa overlooking West Princes Street Gardens. The turret is in the shape of a goose-pie, a term also used because it suggests the amiable cowardice of the plump wigmaker and poet Allan Ramsay (1686–1758), who built the villa as a love-nest for his wife (and as a joint retirement haven). However, in 1745 the building was overrun by fierce Jacobite snipers taking pot-shots at the castle – whose garrison had refused to surrender. Ramsay, a keen golfer, reluctantly took to his heels out of the city to the safety of the countryside:

> Farewell, my bonny, lovely, witty, pretty Maggy,
> And a' the rosy lasses milking on the down;
> Adieu the flowery meadow, aft sae dear to Jocky,
> The sports and merry glee of Edinborrow town.

The Mound

Linking the Old Town and the New, the Mound has a special place in the hearts of Edinburgh citizens, giving access on the one hand to the worlds of religion, banking, the legal system and the theatre and on the other to art galleries, the retail world of Princes Street and the recreational facilities in Princes Street Gardens. The Mound was shaped between 1781 and 1830 from around two million cartloads of earth and building materials removed during the construction of the New Town – a classic example of very productive recycling. Today the Mound provides a gently sloping surface for people in a hurry (such as lawyers or ministers of the cloth) or those enjoying a more leisurely promenade.

Access

An optional diversion down to the north, via the winding slope of the Mound and back up by the more direct Playfair Steps.

Allan Ramsay Statue

Far below his Ramsay Garden villa, at the Princes Street side of Princes Street Gardens, stands the Italian Carrara marble statue of Allan Ramsay, sculpted by Sir John Steell in 1865. On the plinth is a medallion of the Ramsay family. Born in Leadhills, Lanarkshire, Ramsay was first apprenticed to an Edinburgh wigmaker. However, he was so good at writing songs and poems that he started a bookselling business at 155 High Street, selling his own *Scots Songs* (1719), *The Tea-table Miscellany* (1724–37) and his best work, *The Gentle Shepherd* (1725), a play. In 1726

he moved to new premises on the first floor of the narrow Luckenbooth building beside St Giles. So popular was it that his shop was nicknamed the 'Hub of the Universe'. At the Luckenbooths Ramsay set up the first circulating library in Scotland (1725). In 1736 he opened a theatre at Carrubbers Close in the High Street, but it was shut down by the magistrates the following year.

Floral Clock

The Floral Clock was the invention of John McHattie, Edinburgh Parks Superintendent, who first delighted visitors and citizens with his creation in the spring of 1904. It was constructed by Messrs James Ritchie & Sons Ltd from the old turret clock of Elie parish church, Fife, and this mechanism lasted till 1936, when it was first replaced. The mechanism of the clock is in the plinth of the statue of Allan Ramsay. More than 24,000 flowers, dwarf varieties of many colours, are used in the clock; in all, they take about three weeks to plant.

Tactile Edinburgh

Strategically placed between two of Edinburgh's great art galleries, the National Gallery of Scotland and the Royal Scottish Academy, Falmouth artist David Westby's bronze landscape sculpture of the centre of Edinburgh both entertains children and is of enormous benefit to the blind and partially sighted. Situated as it is at the foot of the great Playfair Steps (which form a shortcut up the Mound for the energetic traveller or lawyers hurrying up to the courts of law on the High Street), the model of Edinburgh is a fine example of art with a useful public function, a talking-point as well as a tool. For decades the piazza between the galleries has been Edinburgh's Hyde Park for orators and has also provided a satisfying performance space during the city's rolling programme of festivals.

National Gallery of Scotland (The Mound)

As well as a fine collection of Scottish paintings, the National Gallery has a representative display of European art from the Renaissance to the Impressionists. Every January the gallery's Turner watercolours are exhibited. The new Weston Link offers enhanced gallery space, a restaurant and an enlarged bookshop, as well as good views of East Princes Street Gardens.

Access

At the foot of the Mound.

Royal Scottish Academy (The Mound)

An independent charity, the RSA presents an extensive programme of contemporary Scottish art throughout the year and a revolving display of work from the permanent collection. Open to the public every Monday.

Access

At the foot of the Mound on Princes Street.

CASTLEHILL

Camera Obscura and World of Illusions

Access

A paid attraction on the north side of Castlehill.

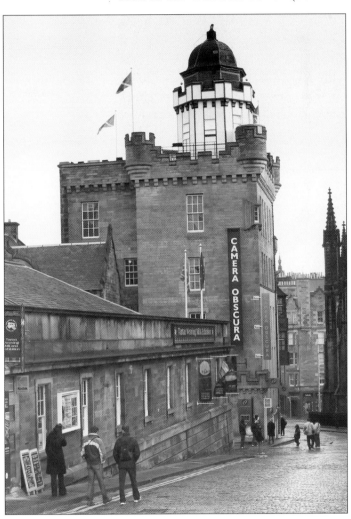

The imaginative hand of town planner Sir Patrick Geddes can again be seen at the Outlook Tower (549 Castle-hill). The lower part of the building dates from the seventeenth century, and was constructed on the site of the mansion of the Laird o' Cockpen (a Ramsay of Dalhousie who gave his name to the nearby Ramsay Garden and an old Scots song 'The Laird o' Cockpen'). The upper floors of the tower were added in 1853 when Maria Theresa Short installed a camera obscura offering panoramic views of the city. In 1896 Geddes reorganised the interior into what he called an 'outlook tower' to show the intimate relationship between geology, vegetation and the human race. At the top, below Short's camera, Geddes also installed a planetarium, with a Scotland Room beneath, followed by surveys of Britain, Europe and the world, with two globes, one showing vegetation and the other geology. Geddes's idea was to alert the general public to the close links between man and his environment, and the importance of conservation. In 1945 an improved lens and mirror system was installed in the camera obscura. Today the camera obscura is one of Edinburgh's most unusual attractions, and is open every day.

Scotch Whisky Centre

Access

A paid attraction on the south side of Castlehill.

An imaginatively designed journey through three hundred years of the history of Scotch whisky, the Scotch Whisky Centre brings to life the intimate connection between land and people, and between the mysterious processes of fermentation and distillation and the restorative effects of Scotland's own 'water of life'.

Boswell's Court

Returning back up the Mound to Castlehill, we begin to absorb the bewildering complexity of the Old Town, its mysterious nooks and shadowy crannies. Crossing the roadway to the southern side of Castlehill we find Boswell's Court, a seventeenth-century five-storey tenement named after the physician uncle of James Boswell (1740–95), Dr Samuel Johnson's biographer. The old stair stands in the passageway to one of Edinburgh's best restaurants, The Witchery, with its enchanting Secret Garden.

Typical of the many interesting corners of the Lawnmarket courts on the northern side of Castlehill is Joe Hagan's basement workshop at 13a James Court, where he makes bagpipes and enjoys explaining the intricacies of the instrument to visitors.

Further down the street stands the venerable Tolbooth St John's Church, designed by James Gillespie Graham (1842–4), towering

Access

On the south side of Castlehill.

majestically over the Lawnmarket. Once the Victoria Hall for the General Assembly of the Established Church, it is now known as The Hub and (with a fine first-floor hall, restaurants and booking office) functions as the social and administrative headquarters of the Edinburgh International Festival. The Festival's roots date back to 1944 and a conversation in a London restaurant in Hanover Square, between the Vienna-born administrator Rudolf Bing and H. Harvey Wood, representative of the British Council. The high ideals of reconciliation and regeneration which the Festival embodied were dramatically seen in the emotional reunion in Edinburgh between the conductor Bruno Walter and his beloved Vienna Philharmonic Orchestra, a reunion which took place at the (first) 1947 Festival in Edinburgh. The immense

Joe Hagan's bagpipe workshop. (*Courtesy of Joe Hagan*)

international popularity of the Festival is shown by the £19.3m generated by the event in 2004.

In front of the church is a circle of cobblestones now used as a traffic roundabout; the cobbles mark the site of the old Weigh House or Butter Tron where butter and cheese were weighed and sold. The first Weigh House was destroyed by an English army in 1384. The 'Over Tron' was often the scene of public festivities. In 1554 on Corpus Christi Day, for example, it was made into a stage for the Craftsmen's Church Play, perfomed in front of Queen Mary of Guise (whose palace faced it across the road). In 1614 the Town Council replaced the Tron with a new one but this building was then demolished by Oliver Cromwell's troops in the castle siege of 1650. Finally in 1660 another Weigh House (whose cellar was also used as a jail) was erected. In 1745 it was taken over by the Jacobites as a guardhouse. In 1822 the Weigh House was demolished to widen the road for the visit of George IV to Edinburgh.

Edinburgh International Festival's The Hub.

Access

Walk south of the roundabout as the road slopes down towards the Grassmarket.

Upper Bow

South of the Assembly Hall, across the road, is the Upper Bow, once the head of a steep zig-zag road leading up from the Grassmarket far below. The Upper Bow was used as an entry and exit by the kings and queens of Scotland and by criminals being taken down to execution. The fun-loving James IV and the superstitious James VI passed this way, as well as Mary, Queen of Scots, her husband James, Earl of Bothwell, and the unfortunate Charles I. Down its cobbles the hated head of the City Guard, Captain John ('Jock') Porteous (who had ordered his men to fire on the crowd during an execution), was dragged to his grisly death in 1736, strung up on a dyer's pole.

Upper Bow shopfronts today.

West Bow

'A perfect Z in figure,' wrote the publisher and historian Robert Chambers of the West Bow, 'composed of tall antique houses, with numerous dovecot-like gables projecting over the footway, full of old inscriptions and sculpturings, presenting at every few steps some darksome lateral profundity, into which the imagination wanders without hindrance or exhaustion.' Further down the sloping street Major Thomas Weir, popularly believed to have been a warlock – at night he was said to gallop through the West Bow on a headless horse – committed his unspeakable deeds. In 1834 the Upper Bow was separated from the West Bow by the construction of Victoria Street and Victoria Terrace.

Grassmarket

The Grassmarket was for long the abode of farriers, fairs and mountebanks; it was a place for horse-trading, sweetmeats and grisly executions – such as those of the hapless Covenanters imprisoned in the late seventeenth century at Greyfriars Kirkyard and then sentenced by Sir George Mackenzie to death by hanging ('Giving Glory to God in the Grassmarket').

But the Grassmarket also had happier and more romantic aspects: at its busy coaching inns such luminaries as the poet Robert Burns (1786–7) and the pianist Franz Liszt (1841) were entertained and gratefully accepted the rapt attentions of the fairer sex. For many years a weekly grain and livestock market was a Grassmarket feature. At the popular Hallow Fair the booths and barrows of the huxters were strategically placed; the smell from scores of paraffin oil jets did not stop the public from consuming large quantities of gingerbread, sliced coconut or black puddings. Ear-splitting shouts and raucous music filled the air from the travelling booths with their human monstrosities, the menageries with their lion-tamers, the Fat Lady, the Living Skeleton, the Punch and Judy man and the 'penny gaffes' (theatre booths) with their crude but grippingly dramatic story-lines.

Access

Continue descending south to Victoria Street far below.

Access

The easterly continuation of the Grassmarket, passing under the North Bridge and then the South Bridge.

Cowgate

Formerly the habitation of cardinals and ambassadors, by the nineteenth century the once-splendid Cowgate had become seedy and disreputable, the unpleasant underbelly of the more prestigious High Street. As the writer Alexander Smith wistfully complained: 'Admired once by a French ambassador at the court of one of the Jameses, and yet with certain traces of departed splendour, the Cowgate has fallen into the sere and yellow leaf [decay] of furniture-brokers, second-hand jewellers and vendors of deleterious alcohol.' Crowding the Cowgate were impoverished Irish migrants, struggling to accommodate themselves to the prudent ways of their Presbyterian host nation. Today, after considerable urban regeneration and a disastrous fire in Guthrie Street, the Cowgate is slowly becoming a more desirable place to live and work. Yet the traces of its former decline still give the Cowgate a touch of mystery and excitement.

The Magdalen Chapel

Access

At 41 Cowgate, beyond the east end of the Grassmarket and almost under the North Bridge.

Founded by Michael Macqueen, a local burgess, in the early years of the sixteenth century, the chapel supported a chaplain and seven poor men living in an attached hospital. In return, their function was to pray for the repose of the soul of Mary, Queen of Scots, for the founder, his wife Janet and their descendants, and for the patrons of the chapel (the Deacon and Masters of the craft of the Hammermen of the City of Edinburgh, whose responsibility the endowment was to in future years). The four pieces of pre-Reformation stained glass in the chapel today once faced a nobleman's garden and so escaped destruction during the Reformation. They are the only examples of pre-Reformation stained glass in Scotland still in their original location. By 1615 only the chapel remained standing and this was adapted by the Hammermen to form a Convening Hall. It was decorated in 1725 with the painted coats of armsof the eight trades included in the Incorporation of Hammermen (pew-terers, lorimers, saddlers, blacksmiths, cutlers, locksmiths, armourers and shearsmiths). The chapel was the meeting-place of the first General Assembly of the Church of Scotland(20 December 1560) with forty-two members (only six of whom were ministers, including John Knox, as no moderator had been chosen). Today, although the chapel is privately owned (as the headquarters of the Scottish Reformation Society), it is open to the general public (Tel: 0131 220 1450).

(Crown copyright: RCAHMS)

Access

Return from the
Grassmarket to the
Royal Mile.

LAWNMARKET

Two explanations have been put forward for the word Lawnmarket: first, as the only location in the Old Town where traders from outside the burgh could sell their wares ('land market'), and secondly, as the location where linen (lawn) was permitted to be sold. Generally, like most Edinburgh streets, it had an unsavoury reputation. In 1773 the lexicographer and critic Dr Samuel Johnson, while walking up the Lawnmarket to James' Court, arm-in-arm with his biographer James Boswell, made his cutting aside on the subject of the customary waste disposal arrangements in the Old Town, which involved throwing 'night soil' from a great height into the street. 'It was a dusky night,' writes Boswell, 'I could not prevent his being assailed by the evening effluvia of Edinburgh.' Dr Johnson's only reaction was the acid riposte, 'I smell you in the dark.' Human waste thus ejected was also commonly (and sarcastically) referred to as 'the flowers o' Edinburgh'.

Once the Edinburgh lands (tenements) housed both rich and poor, who were separated from each other by a hierarchy of floors but were obliged to rub shoulders on the stairs. The nobility would be on the first floor, the professionals (lawyers and doctors) on the second, the merchants on the third, the working classes on the fourth and the poor and destitute on the ramshackle top storey, frozen by the biting east wind.

(Copyright: F.C. Inglis)

But in later years all this changed. Writing in the 1870s Robert Louis Stevenson describes with atmospheric skill the condition of an Old Town tenement after the rich and the noble had moved north to the more airy and genteel squares and crescents of the New Town: 'In one house two-score families herd together. The great hotel is given over to discomfort from the foundation to chimney-tops. In the first room there is a birth, in another a death, in a third a sordid drinking-bout, and the detective and the Bible reader cross upon the stairs. Social inequality is nowhere more ostentatious than at Edinburgh.'

Access

On the north side of the Lawnmarket.

Mylne's Court

While Edinburgh's sun-splashed courts provide stages for pigeons to strut on, at night they are as full of intrigue as any Italian medieval city. Crossing to the north side of the High Street the visitor finds Mylne's Court, built by royal master mason Robert Mylne (1633–1710), the seventh member of his family to hold that exalted position; their magnificent family burial ground can still be seen in the grounds of the Greyfriars Kirk. In 1745, during the occupation of Edinburgh by Prince Charlie's forces, Mylne's Court housed some of the officers of the Jacobite army. In 1883 the west side of the court was demolished but in the late 1960s the south block and the east range were rebuilt by Edinburgh University as student accommodation.

James' Court

To the north, below the rear of the Assembly Hall of the Church of Scotland, is the wide expanse of James' Court. Built by James Brownhill in 1727, it was the residence of well-off burgesses and its garden was planted with shady lime trees. The philosopher David Hume (1711–76) lived on the third storey of the west stair from 1762. While Hume was in France (1763–6), Dr Hugh Blair (1718–1800), the fastidious Professor of Rhetoric and Belles Lettres, lived in Hume's house. Dr Blair's favourite reading was *The Arabian Nights* and *Don Quixote*; he was a very careful dresser, even placing a mirror flat on the floor and standing on tip-toe over it to look over his shoulder at the cut of his coat. In 1773 James Boswell was tenant of the house, where, on 14 August, he received Dr Johnson. The portly doctor at that time had given up alcoholic drink. When he arrived at Boyd's Inn (off St Mary's Street in the Canongate) he asked the waiter to bring some sugar to sweeten his lemonade. The waiter picked up a lump of sugar in his greasy fingers and plopped it into the glass. The doctor, in a fury, threw the lemonade, glass and all, straight out of the open window!

Access

On the north side of the Lawnmarket, approached by three entrances (West, Mid and East).

Gladstone's Land

Gladstone's Land dates partly from before the sixteenth century. When Thomas Gledstanes and his wife bought it in 1617 the front of the stone and timber building was then over 20 feet behind the present outer arches. This was the year when King James VI finally came back to the Edinburgh he had left in 1603 when taking over the English throne as James I. The year 1617 was a time of great rejoicing in Edinburgh and

Access

On the north side of the Lawnmarket.

the king's visit signalled an immediate expansion in self-confidence and prosperity. Gledstanes built out 23 feet from the house as he found it, doing away with the intimate wooden galleries on the floors above. Other property owners did the same, so decreasing the width of the High Street with fashionable and solid stone fronts (which were less

vulnerable to fire than the old wooden ones) and arcades for shelter from the weather. Visitors to the building went up the 'fore-stair' from the pavement and then up the narrow turnpike. Often the fore-stair was used to shelter livestock, hens or pigs (although pigs were also known to have been kept on the top floor of some tenements). Edinburgh is sometimes credited with the invention of the skyscraper. Because of the crag-and-tail slope of the High Street, houses often rose to six storeys on the street front (like Gladstone's Land) but had as many as fifteen to the rear. The property is now in the hands of the National Trust for Scotland and is open to the general public (except during the winter). The fine golden hawk launching itself from the building is a pun on the family name 'Gladstone', a *gled* being the Scots word for hawk.

Lady Stair's Close

Access

No. 477 Lawnmarket, or from the Mound.

Lady Stair's House was completed in 1622 and later re-created in 1895 for Lord Rosebery. Originally the house was in a cul-de-sac and had been the home of Elizabeth, Dowager Countess of Stair (d. 1759), a shining light in Edinburgh polite society in the early eighteenth century. Her first husband was Viscount Primrose, a man with a violent temper who treated her badly. One day she was in her bedroom looking into her mirror when she saw her husband creeping up behind her, a sword in his hand. Fearing for her life, she jumped out of the window into the street below. Soon afterwards, Lord Primrose went abroad. Some time later a fortune-teller came to Edinburgh. Lady Primrose, disguised as a servant, consulted him for news of her husband. The fortune-teller took her to a large mirror where she saw her husband walking up the aisle of a church with a young bride at his side. Suddenly she saw her brother walk forward and attack her husband with his sword – but she saw no more. Months later her brother returned from abroad and confirmed the details of what she had seen in the fortune-teller's mirror. The historian and publisher Robert Chambers tells this tale, and Sir Walter Scott used it for one of his best short stories ('My Aunt

Margaret's Mirror'). Today the building houses one of the best City of Edinburgh Council's local museums, the Writers' Museum, devoted to the life and work of Sir Walter Scott, Robert Burns and Robert Louis Stevenson.

Riddell's Court

Access

On the south side of the Lawnmarket.

At 322 Riddell's Court is Bailie Macmorran's House. In 1593 James VI and his queen, Anne of Denmark, banqueted with Danish nobles at the home of the unfortunate Macmorran, who is remembered as the town official who was killed two years later outside Edinburgh's High School with a bullet fired by a rioting schoolboy. In later years the philosopher David Hume lived here before moving across the road to James' Court. The pensive bust of Socrates was installed by the town planner Sir

Patrick Geddes. Today the educational theme is continued (if more peacefully than in Macmorran's day) as the court houses an adult basic education unit and the Workers' Educational Association.

Access

On the south side of the Lawnmarket.

Brodie's Close

Visiting Edinburgh in 1895, the London-born novelist Israel Zangwill (1864–1926) was overcome by the duplicity of the environment. For him, Edinburgh was a whited sepulchre, a breeding-ground of crime and evil: 'Those sunless courts, entered by needles' eyes of apertures, congested

with hellish, heaven-scaling barracks, reeking with refuse and evil odours, inhabited promiscuously by poverty and prostitution.' Perhaps Zangwill was remembering Deacon Brodie (the two-faced model for Stevenson's *Dr Jekyll and Mr Hyde*). Brodie's father was a respected cabinet-maker in the Lawnmarket and a member of the Town Council. His son William succeeded to the business in 1780 and soon became a leading deacon of the town councillors. But he had acquired a taste for gambling and a reputation for cheating with loaded dice – a side of his character that he kept well hidden from his unsuspecting customers, pretending to be an upright citizen. In 1787 a series of daylight robberies took place in Edinburgh in which premises were broken into and goods disappeared as if by magic. In fact it was Brodie, who had made duplicate keys from the masters supplied by the customers for whom he was making furniture. More of Brodie's story appears on p. 71 – but he may be the only man to have been hanged on a wooden gallows that he had constructed himself. Across the road is a well-known pub named after Brodie.

New College (diversion to north)

To some, Edinburgh is visibly scarred by the battle between vice and virtue, and never more so than in the many religious struggles which were fought through the city churches and streets. 'A whole serpent-brood of evils, a gorgon's head held up in the sight of the new towns-men, turning their hearts to stone,' said Sir Patrick Geddes many years later about the Old Town.

The instigator of the greatest religious revolution Scotland has ever seen, John Knox (c. 1513–72), was born in East Lothian. First a Catholic priest and papal notary, he became committed to religious reform after the execution of the Protestant martyr George Wishart in 1546 at the hands of Cardinal David Beaton, himself murdered in revenge at St Andrews three months later. The following year Knox came to the town to work as a Protestant minister. When St Andrews Castle surrendered to the French some weeks later, Knox was imprisoned as a galley-slave. Two years later he was released at the request of King Edward VI of England and began to take an active part in the English Reformation. Having been made a royal chaplain, Knox was offered a bishopric but turned it down. When Archbishop Cranmer was drawing up his Articles of Religion, Knox was one of his consultants, as he was over the writing of the Second Prayer Book in 1552. During the reign of the Catholic Queen Mary, Knox returned to the continent. He was minister to the English exiles in Frankfurt and in Geneva (where he met John Calvin), to the radical reformers opposed to the English settlement. In 1559 Knox was recalled to Scotland. By 1560 the Estates (Scottish Parliament) had decided on religious reform. Knox and five assistants prepared a Confession of Faith which repudiated papal jurisdiction and forbade the celebration of the Catholic mass. Next came Knox's *Book of Discipline*

Access

At the top of the Mound, reached either directly via Lady Stair's Close or more circuitously by Bank Street. Today New College is part of Edinburgh University and the Assembly Hall is administered by the Church of Scotland. Public access is permitted to the courtyard and also to the Assembly Hall when it houses events such as theatrical performances or open conferences.

(By permission of Edinburgh University)

which outlined a non-episcopal form of church government and a national plan for universal education from parish school to university, as well as a systematic programme of poor relief to fill the gap left by the running-down of the monasteries and the expulsion of the religious orders. When Queen Mary returned to Scotland in 1561 she immediately had the Catholic mass celebrated once again. John Knox challenged Mary on many occasions, disputing her version of Christianity. He had already shown his disapproval of women rulers in general in his *First Blast of the Trumpet against the Monstrous Regiment of Women*, a publication which even Queen Elizabeth of England never forgave. Nevertheless, Knox moved to England in 1566 but returned to Scotland in 1572, where he preached for the last time at St Giles Kirk and died shortly afterwards. In his epitaph on Knox the Regent Morton commented: 'Here lies one who neither flattered nor feared any flesh.'

Contained within the New College complex is the Assembly Hall of the Church of Scotland, home to the General Assembly where, during the Edinburgh International Festival, some of the world's finest plays have been presented by the greatest actors, such as Claire Bloom, Christopher Plummer and Sir Ian McKellen.

HIGH STREET

The section of the Royal Mile from George IV Bridge to the Netherbow Port is known as the 'High Street'; this is doubly accurate as not only are the buildings all several storeys high but the roadway itself is high above sea-level. The Royal Mile itself is often said to be like the skeleton of a flat-fish: the castle is the head, the Royal Mile the spine, with the Closes as the bones, and Holyroodhouse as the tail. Others have seen in it a 'strong rhinoceros skin' (Thomas Carlyle) or thought of it as 'a huge lizard' (Alexander Smith). It is Edinburgh's ability to conjure up emotion (both positive and negative) which gives the city its enduring power.

In Libberton's Wynd (now demolished), which once ran near the line of George IV Bridge on the south side of the High Street, the sentimental novelist Henry Mackenzie (author of *The Man of Feeling*) was born in 1745; the Wynd was also the site of the famous John Dowie's tavern, whose biggest room held fourteen persons and the smallest ('The Coffin') six at a pinch. David Hume frequented the tavern, Robert Burns found consolation in 'The Coffin' in 1786 (as his admired but unfortunate predecessor Robert Fergusson also had), and the portrait-painter Sir Henry Raeburn was often to be found there. The beer served in the tavern was Archibald Younger's ale, 'a potent fluid, which almost glued the lips of the drinker together and of which few, therefore, could dispatch more than a bottle', wrote publisher Robert Chambers. The speciality of the house was Nor' Loch trout – haddock stuffed and fried in breadcrumbs.

Access

On Bank Street above
the Mound.

Bank of Scotland

Another brief diversion north from the High Street leads down Bank
Street to the imposing headquarters of the Bank of Scotland, the original
1806 structure rebuilt in 1863 by David Bryce (with additions such as a
'Cyclops Eye' window).

Returning to the High Street the first building on the north side is the
High Court of Justiciary (built in 1937), where a very wide variety of
criminal cases is dealt with; the Sheriff Court, which formerly occupied
the building, has moved to nearby Chambers Street. In front of the
High Court stands the statue of the philosopher David Hume by the
sculptor Sandy Stoddart (1997).

Parliament Square

Up to the nineteenth century Parliament Square was a warren of rickety booths and workshops precariously attached to the walls of St Giles High Kirk. Parliament Close was full of booksellers, watch-makers, goldsmiths (such as George Heriot) and coffee-shops where much legal business was transacted. The most famous coffee-shop was that of Peter Williamson (1730–99). 'Indian Peter' had been kidnapped at the age of eight from his home town of Aberdeen and sold as a slave in Philadelphia. During his time in America he was captured and scalped by Indians and taken prisoner by the French. Williamson eventually obtained his freedom, became a planter and then returned to Edinburgh where he opened a coffee-house and a tavern. He was also a printer, publisher and bookseller. Williamson started the first penny post in Edinburgh and brought out the first Edinburgh street directory. He is buried in the Old Calton cemetery.

Access

At the front of the west door of St Giles High Kirk.

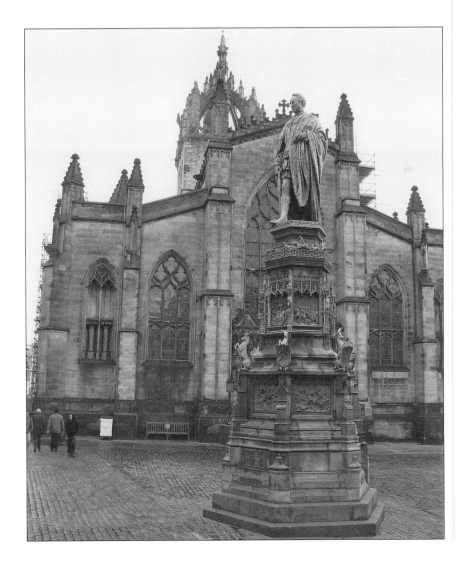

Parliament Hall

Parliament Hall has a fine collection of sculptures and a number of paintings. The Great South Window installed in 1868 shows the inauguration of the Court of Session and College of Justice by James V on 27 May 1532. The window was designed and made at the Royal Bavarian Glass Factory in Munich, one of Edinburgh's twin cities.

Following the union of the parliaments (1707) the venerable Parliament House lost its legislative role and became instead the legal heart of Scotland, with the High Court of Justiciary (the supreme criminal court) and the Court of Session (the supreme civil court), the Signet and Advocates' Libraries. The hammerbeam roof of Parliament Hall is of Danish oak and was installed in 1639. From 1707 (when the Parliament was dissolved), the hall has been given over exclusively to the needs of the Scottish law courts, now located across the High Street.

Visiting Parliament Hall in 1867 Thomas Carlyle gave the following description of the scene: 'An immense Hall, dimly lighted from the top of the walls, and perhaps with candles burning in it here and there; all in strange chiaroscuro, and filled with what I thought a thousand or two of human creatures; all astir in a boundless buzz of talk, and simmering about in every direction, some solitary, some in groups. By degrees I

(Copyright: F.C. Inglis)

noticed that some were in wig and black gown, some not, but in common clothes, all well-dressed; that here and there on the sides of the Hall, were little thrones with enclosures, and steps leading up; red-velvet figures sitting in said thrones, and the black-gowned eagerly speaking to them – Advocates pleading to Judges.' By 1808 Henry, Lord Cockburn complained of the Inner House that 'it was impossible to say whether it had ever been painted'.

St Giles High Kirk

St Giles is the parish church of Edinburgh, built soon after the town received burgh status in 1130. For centuries the church and its bells were a familiar landmark in the city. The fifteenth-century poet-priest William Dunbar wrote affectionately, 'Fra sound of St Giles bell/Never think I to flee,' but by the eighteenth century the poet Robert Fergusson dismissed the chime as a 'Wanworthy [useless], crazy, dinsome thing'. Although the twelfth-century north doorway with its Romanesque decoration survived till the 1790s, there is now virtually no trace of the original building except one scallop capital and a recently discovered corbel carved with the face of an animal. At the time of the Reformation the formerly revered relic of St Giles was given to the Dean of Guild, the wooden statue of the saint was carried in procession to the Nor'

Access

St Giles is a working church which visitors are encouraged to enter; during church services, however, the normal casual tourist activities are not permitted. Visitors should be guided by the church officer and beadles and should generally exercise restraint and consideration, given the nature and purpose of the building.

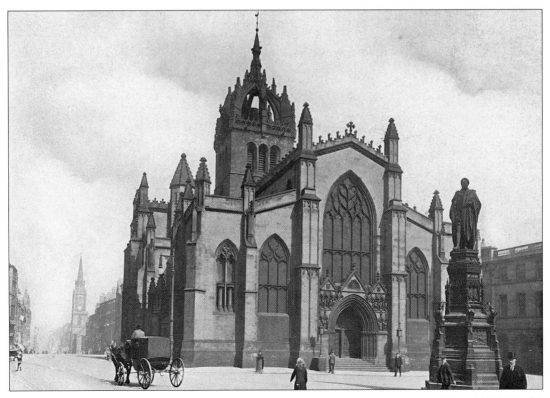

(Copyright: F.C. Inglis)

Loch (on the site of the present Princes Street Gardens) and unceremoniously dumped into the water, while the church's gold and silver vessels were sold and the proceeds used for the benefit of the town. The medieval screens and furnishings were destroyed, the forty-four altars in the church removed and the privately owned compartments taken away to make one big communal church. However, this created more room than the congregation needed and so the Town Council used part of the west end as a new Tolbooth and the east end as a school.

For four months in 1571 the steeple of St Giles was fortified and held by troops loyal to Mary, Queen of Scots. By 1572 John Knox, the minister of St Giles, was 'so weak that he had to be lifted into the pulpit by two servants'. As religious needs changed the church was subdivided again and by 1578 three separate congregations worshipped there. When Charles I made St Giles into a cathedral in 1633 under the loathed episcopal system of bishops with its elaborate ceremonials and English liturgies, much alteration took place and the church once again lost its subdivisions.

Popular resistance came to a head in 1637 when Jenny Geddes, a High Street vegetable seller, picked up a folding-stool during one of the new services and threw it straight at the dean as he stood up in the pulpit. Curiously, the subdivisions of the church returned in 1639 and were in existence in various combinations until finally removed in 1882 under a scheme of renovation initiated by Lord Provost William Chambers.

St Giles – Marquess of Montrose Monument

James Graham, Marquess of Montrose (1612–50), who had fought against the Covenanters but was finally captured and executed at the Mercat Cross, had his body disposed of as he had himself so poignantly predicted:

> Let them bestow on ev'ry Airth a Limb:
> Open all my Veins, that I may swim
> To Thee my Saviour, in that Crimson Lake;
> Then place my pur-boil'd Head upon a Stake;
>
> Scatter my Ashes, throw them in the Air:
> Lord since Thou know'st where all these Atoms are
> I'm hopeful, once Thou'lt recollect my Dust,
> And confident Thou'lt raise me with the Just.

Access

The monument is in the south-east side of the church in the Chepman Aisle.

(By permission of St Giles Cathedral)

The white marble effigy lying on the tomb in full armour and holding a sword is still the object of great local affection, as the red roses regularly placed there keenly testify.

Heart of Midlothian

A heart-shaped Edinburgh icon formed with coloured granite setts (cobblestones) marks the spot where once glowered the Old Tolbooth gaol with its hated condemned cell. Brass plates still show the outlines of the Old Tolbooth and the Luckenbooths which were built up against it. The Heart of Midlothian also marks the doorway out of the gaol. The

custom was for prisoners who had been set free to spit as they passed
through the door and out to liberty. The hated symbol of the Old
Tolbooth stands near the execution platform. The historian Hugh
Arnot, writing in 1778, described the cells of the Old Tolbooth: 'In the
corner of the room we saw, shoved together, a quantity of dust, rags and
straw, the refuse of a long succession of criminals. We went to the
apartment above, where were two miserable boys, not twelve years of
age. But there we had no leisure for observation; for, no sooner was the
door opened, than such an incredible stench assailed us, from the
stagnant and putrid air, as utterly to overpower us.'

Sir Walter Scott was present in 1817 to watch the demolition of the
Old Tolbooth and the condemned cell – a strong oak chest, iron-plated,
9 feet square, closed by an iron door with heavy bolts and locks. The
young engineer James Nasmyth, who was also there with his father and
Scott (a friend of his father), wrote: 'As soon as the clouds of dust had
been dispersed, he observed, under the place where the iron box had
stood, a number of skeletons of rats, as dry as mummies. He [James
Nasmyth] selected one of these, wrapped it in a newspaper, and put it in
his pocket, as a recollection of his first day in Edinburgh and of the total
destruction of the "Heart of Midlothian".'

After the demolition of the Old Tolbooth, Sir Walter acquired its
iron-studded door and took it to Abbotsford, his home in the Borders,
setting it into a wall on the house roof. Although the name today
belongs to one of Scotland's biggest football teams, Muriel Spark, the
Edinburgh-born novelist, later described the symbolic heart as 'the
saturnine Heart of Midlothian, never mine!'

Luckenbooths and Krames

Access

The outline of the buildings can still be seen in brass plates set into the High Street.

The Luckenbooths – permanent lockable shops with wooden shutters – ran along the middle of the High Street north of St Giles, forming the 'Stinking Stile', a narrow defile down the side of the Kirk, thick with mud and slops. Although the Luckenbooths were mainly permanent shops the west end of the long, tall and thin cluster of buildings was formed by the Old Tolbooth, built in around 1386 and used variously as a meeting-place for the Scottish Parliament, for the Town Council, as a tax collection office and, most memorably, as the town gaol, until its momentous demolition in 1817. The Luckenbooths dated from about 1460 and consisted of seven timber tenements between four and six storeys high. In 1728 Allan Ramsay opened the first circulating library in Britain on the first floor of the east end of the Luckenbooths and fifty-eight years later William Creech, publisher and book-seller, set up his premises immediately below.

But today the fabled Luckenbooths no longer exist; they are purely symbolic. They are remembered chiefly for the charming Luckenbooth Brooch, a silver ornament made of two intertwined hearts in the form of the letter M, thought to be related to romantic stories which grew up about the life of Mary, Queen of Scots.

> As I went by the Luckenbooths
> I saw a lady fair;
> She had long ear-rings in her ears
> And jewels in her hair.

The Krames (probably a Dutch word) first appeared in 1550. They were temporary stalls for selling goods. Lord Cockburn remembers that 'their little stands, each enclosed in a tiny room of its own, and during the day all open to the little footpath that ran between the two rows of them, and all glittering with attractions, contained everything fascinating to childhood, but chiefly toys. It was like one of the Arabian Nights' bazaars in Baghdad. The Krames was the paradise of childhood.'

Charles II Statue

The oldest equestrian lead statue of its kind in Britain, the 6-ton figure of Charles II on horseback was first erected in 1685 at a cost of £2,580. Robert Louis Stevenson caricatured it as 'a bandy-legged and garlanded Charles Second made of lead, bestrides a tun-bellied charger'.

Ironically, the 'Merry Monarch' sits high above the grave of the great Reformer John Knox, marked in parking bay no. 23 by a beige square, opposite a stained-glass window in the nearby wall of St Giles with the Latin initials of the great Reformer *(IK)*.

Mercat Cross

'Here I stand at what is called the Mercat Cross of Edinburgh, and can in a few minutes take fifty men of genius and learning by the hand' – so claimed (perhaps extravagantly) Mr Amyat, the king's chemist, as recorded by the editor of the *Encyclopaedia Britannica*, William Smellie (1740–95), a remark which emphasises the importance of the Mercat (merchant or trading) Cross as an officially designated place of public sale, bargaining and purchase. Today the cross consists of a wide octagonal base (with steps for sitting on or resting containers), a platform above (for public proclamations), fitted with spouts for drain-age or for pouring wine out on festive occasions, and, at the top of the tall stone shaft, a painted heraldic device and a

cross (intended as a reminder of the need for fairness and sincerity in business transactions).

The Mercat Cross was also an easily recognisable place to meet and, inevitably, the haunt of gossips and *cadies* (carriers). Opposite Fishmarket Close (on the south side) a large circle of cobbles marks the former location of the Mercat Cross, first erected in the twelfth century in the middle of the High Street on a line between the present cross and the City Chambers. This medieval cross was taken down in 1617 and moved east to the head of Fleshmarket Close. In 1756 the cross was demolished to widen the road for traffic (the new Royal Exchange had made it redundant) and it was not till 1885 that the present cross was erected by William Gladstone, some yards to the west – where it now stands in Parliament Square. At the Mercat Cross state proclamations were made of the death of kings and to hail their successors, and it is said that on the night before the Scots' defeat at Flodden in 1513 ghostly heralds were seen proclaiming the names of the ten thousand who would die in the battle.

At the cross, too, state criminals were executed (such as Montrose, Huntly, the Argylls and Warriston), and the banners of the Highland clans defeated at Culloden in 1745 were burnt by the public executioner.

Byres Close

Visible from Advocate's Close is the tall, wedge-shaped mansion of Adam Bothwell (*c.* 1530–93), Bishop of Orkney and Commendator (lay administrator) of Holyrood Abbey. Bothwell, a Roman Catholic career priest with an instinct for survival, married Mary, Queen of Scots to the Earl of Bothwell in May 1567 and (as a Protestant) crowned James

Access

No. 373 on the north side of the High Street.

VI at Stirling two months later. Sir William Dick (1580–1655), a wealthy merchant trading from the Baltic to the Mediterranean (and Provost of Edinburgh in 1638), was a later tenant. According to Robert Chambers, during his occupation of Edinburgh Oliver Cromwell was in the habit of sitting in the north window-bay, scrutinising his navy on manoeuvres out in the River Forth. When the building was restored in 1977 six earthenware pots were found set into the wall; these are thought to be 'acoustic jars' positioned so as to improve the acoustics of the house for private musical concerts.

Advocate's Close

Access

No. 357, north side of the High Street.

The names of houses in the Old Town changed over the years as different occupiers came and went, so one house could have many names from generation to generation. Advocate's Close is named after one particular person: Sir James Stewart (1635–1713), Lord Advocate. It was also the home of Andrew Crosbie (the model for Sir Walter Scott's Councillor Pleydell in his novel *Guy Mannering*) and of Sir John Scougall, a court painter during the reign of William and Mary. It offers a unique view of the New Town from the High Street pavement.

City Chambers

The Royal Exchange was built to give a covered area for city merchants to conduct their business in a more leisurely manner after the unsavoury but exciting scrabble of wheeling and dealing outside at the Mercat Cross. It is the only eighteenth-century building still in the High Street and in its heyday had shops and coffee-houses (where real negotiations could take place) and a Customs House. Today, as the City Chambers, the building functions as the seat of local government, housing the City of Edinburgh Council.

From the beginning the Exchange was associated with eating and drinking as well as commerce. A fascinating insight into the eating habits of the eighteenth-century bourgeois citizens of Edinburgh can be found in the Convivial Records of the Trained Bands of Edinburgh. The Trained Bands were a civil defence organisation drawn from the district wards of the city. On 20 December 1771 fifteen stalwarts sat down for a celebration supper at the Exchange Coffee-House in the courtyard of what is now the City Chambers. They consumed 20 bottles of claret, 4 bottles of port, 8 of port in negus, 2½ mutchkins of punch, 1 bottle of Geneva, 6 bottles of porter, bread and beer, biscuits and cheese and 200 pickled oysters. On 4 June six years later the Society of Captains, consisting of twenty-nine gentlemen, feasted on oranges, apples, almonds, raisins, 25½ pints of claret, 5 bottles of port, 4 bottles of sherry, 2 bottles of hock, 1 bottle of port in negus, porter and brandy, small beer and bread, olives, anchovies and prawns. Four glasses were broken in the games of cards which followed, and a number of the company had to be taken home by the ever-present *cadies*. One gentle-man had to be ferried home in a sedan-chair.

Access

North side of the High Street. Visitors may go to the enquiry desk inside the City Chambers.

(By permission of City of Edinburgh Council)

Mary King's Close

Before leaving the City Chambers the visitor is recommended to visit Mary King's Close, sunk deep below ground level. The Royal Exchange (City Chambers) was built over the cobbled surface of the old close, which had been unoccupied for many years as it was thought that the shops and houses were haunted by those who had died in the plague epidemic of 1644–6. But there were other terrifying episodes in the history of the close. In the late eighteenth century a woman was sitting in her house in Mary King's Close reading her Bible when she looked up and saw a ghostly head floating in the room. Although her husband did not at first believe her, he eventually also saw the head and then a child and an arm. The room filled with ghastly figures, then suddenly there was a hollow groaning and everything vanished.

Today it is possible to join a guided party down into the Close and see exactly what Edinburgh's High Street was like in those far-off days. The Real Mary King's Close conducts tours throughout the year.

(By permission of the Real Mary King's Close)

Fish, Posts and Printing

Access

North side of the High Street under entry arches.

A plaque at the entry to the City Chambers recalls that the house of Sir Simon Preston of Craigmillar (Provost in 1566–7) once stood on that spot. On 15 June 1567 Mary, Queen of Scots spent her last night in Edinburgh at the house after her army's defeat at Carberry (to the east of the city). On the following evening she was removed to Holyrood and later taken north to Lochleven Castle. These were the first steps towards her long imprisonment and eventual death, so poignantly recalled two centuries later by the poet Robert Burns:

> Oh! Soon, to me, may summer-suns
> Nae mair light up the morn!
> Nae mair, to me, the autumn winds
> Wave o'er the yellow corn!
> And in the narrow house o' death
> Let winter round me rave;
> And the next flow'rs, that deck the spring,
> Bloom on my peaceful grave!

(By permission of City of Edinburgh Council)

Access

No. 190, south side of
the High Street.

Old Fishmarket Close

Crossing the High Street to the south side we find Old Fishmarket
Close, which was ravaged by two great fires in 1700 and 1824. The old
buildings (which rose to fifteen storeys at the rear) were destroyed as far
down as the Tron Kirk and replaced with houses of much reduced
proportions. The fishmarket was also the scene of an extraordinary
incident on Hogmanay 1571 when cannon-balls shot from the castle
landed in the fishmarket, throwing shoals of fish up on to the rooftops!

In the nineteenth century, according to Lord Cockburn, the close was
not the most hygienic of places: 'The fish were generally thrown out on
the street at the head of the close, whence they were dragged down by
dirty boys or dirtier women; and then sold unwashed, for there was not a
drop of water in the place, from old rickety, scaly, wooden tables,
exposed to all the rain, dust and filth.'

Police Information Centre

A working police station and police museum, with fascinating exhibits on Burke and Hare, Deacon Brodie and Werner Wälti (a German spy captured at Waverley station by Chief Inspector Willie Merrilees disguised as a railway porter); also on view is a variety of offensive weapons and the old flogging-bench (complete with birch).

Access

Open during the day at 188 High Street.
Tel: 0131 226 6966

Edinburgh Festival Fringe

The Fringe was born as a piratical counter-culture to the more serious dignity of the official Edinburgh International Festival. Over the years, unfettered by Festival directors (and often rebelling against the initial disapproval of some of the City Fathers), the Fringe exploded like a firecracker through the Old Town and the New. The Fringe has been the seed-bed for many a comic or dramatic talent, blending all the arts in a fruitful anarchy only possible within the byzantine nooks and crannies of Edinburgh old and new. Today the Edinburgh Festival Fringe is perhaps older and slightly wiser, but its iconoclasm and sheer zest for life (strikingly symbolised by the zany exterior of the Fringe office) make it the biggest generator of income (£70m in 2004) of all the city's summer festivals.

Access

No. 180, a public office on the south side of the High Street.

Craig's Close

Access

No. 265, north side of
the High Street.

In Craig's Close stood the workshop of publisher Andrew Hart, who brought out an edition of the Bible in 1610. Other publishers and printers lived there in later years: Provost William Creech, Archibald Constable and William Smellie, whose premises were visited by Burns and by Scott. Craig's Close also housed Currie's Tavern, whose specialities were 'pap-in' (beer and whisky curried with oatmeal) and 'het-pint' (mulled wine topped with whipped white of egg).

During the reign of George I (1714–27) Old Post Office Close, as its name implies, was the site of the first post office in Edinburgh. At that time one man delivered letters for the whole of the Old Town.

Anchor Close

Access

No. 241, north side of
the High Street.

Anchor Close was the printing-house of William Smellie (1740–95), where he brought out the first edition of the *Encyclopaedia Britannica* (1781) and, with William Creech, the second 1787 (Edinburgh) edition of Robert Burns' poems. Also in the Close was the notorious Anchor Tavern owned by Dawnay Douglas. The visitor 'found himself in a large kitchen – a dark, fiery Pandemonium, through which numerous ineffable ministers of flame were continually flying about'. Dawnay's wife could be seen in her enormous head-dress, her gown decorated with daisies the size of sunflowers and tulips as big as cabbages. This was the meeting-place of the Crochallan Fencibles, a mock-military organisation named after a Gaelic song that was the proprietor's favourite. William Smellie, founder of the club, introduced Robert Burns to the membership after editing sessions at his publishing house nearby. The parents of Sir Walter Scott lived in the close until 1771.

Geddes Entry

Descending eastwards, the next close the visitor encounters is Geddes Entry (no. 233 north). This was the meeting-place of the Cape Club. Founded in about 1793, the club numbered men of rank and talent in its membership, including the tragedy-struck poet Robert Fergusson, the actor William Wood and the painter Alexander Runciman.

Access

No. 233, north side of the High Street.

North Foulis Close

North Foulis Close housed two of Edinburgh's greatest characters. On the ground floor was the shop of James Gillespie (1726–97), a snuff-grinder and philanthropist who left a fortune to set up one of Edinburgh's best-known schools. It was while a pupil at James Gillespie's School for Girls that the novelist Dame Muriel Spark gathered the material which she would draw on for *The Prime of Miss Jean Brodie*.

On the first floor of the close lived (and died) the inimitable barber and caricaturist John Kay (1742–1826), whose wickedly perceptive etchings of Edinburgh folk were published in his *Edinburgh Portraits*.

Access

No. 299, north side of the High Street.

Old Stamp Office Close

Immediately east is Old Stamp Office Close. This was the location of Fortune's Tavern, where the Lord High Commissioner of 1754 held levées (morning meetings) and from where he walked in state to St Giles Kirk. The tavern was also the meeting-place of the Poker Club (which supported the setting-up of a militia for Scotland). The New (known today as the Royal) Bank had its offices in the close from its institution in 1727 until 1753.

Access

No. 221, north side of the High Street.

Access

South side of the High
Street and various other
locations.

Police Telephone Boxes

Still to be found around Edinburgh are the (now inoperational) blue
police boxes, some brought back to life by being painted dark red and
converted into attractive coffee kiosks. Originally introduced in 1933
(and now on an official preservation listing), the boxes are made of iron
and weigh around 2 tonnes. They were designed by Edinburgh's city
architect Ebenezer MacRae, and have for long been a familiar and
comforting feature of the Edinburgh city landscape.

Access

South side of the High
Street.

The Tron Kirk

On the south side of the Royal Mile the tall grey steeple of the Tron
Kirk points skywards; now plaintively seeking a new lease of life, the
building periodically functions as an Old Town information centre. Built
in 1636–47 by John Mylne (1611–67) to accommodate the Presbyterians
ousted from St Giles when it became an Episcopalian Cathedral under
Charles I, the Tron was so named after the public weighing beam used
to measure salt which stood there. The Tron Kirk was constructed over
the original Marlin's Wynd (said to include the grave of Jean Merlion,
the imported French causeway expert who first paved the High Street).

In the great fire of 1824 the wooden Tron steeple was burnt and the stonework later had to be demolished. W.M. Gilbert wrote of the conflagration:

> On Tuesday fore-noon November 16th, 1824, when all danger seemed to be past, the steeple of the Tron Church was discovered to be on fire. Some burning embers had been carried to the balustrade, and had been fanned into a flame by the wind, which, though it had been calm all night, was by now blowing a gale. The steeple was of wood cased in lead, and blazed furiously. The firemen had to fly for their lives, for the molten lead poured down the sides of the structure, and rendered it impossible to approach it with safety. The heat was so great that a large bell weighing two tons, which had been hung in 1673, was fused. The steeple burned for three-quarters of an hour, and then fell with a crash.

Today the foundations of the restored Tron have been excavated to reveal the early shape of the High Street and the method of street-paving adopted by the early road engineers.

Traditionally the Tron has been the favourite spot for merry-makers to see in the New Year, as can be seen in the illustration.

Some of the most recent discoveries nearby are the vaults under the South Bridge. Identified and excavated in 1985, the vaults are part of the nineteen arches of the South Bridge. In the early nineteenth century they housed an illegal whisky still and probably a brothel. It is also thought that the body-snatchers Burke and Hare used the vaults to store the bodies they had dug up after burial or the victims of their criminal assaults, carried out in the name of medical research.

St Cecilia's Hall and Museum of Instruments

An interesting diversion can be made south down Niddry Street to St Cecilia's Hall, which has its origin in the St Cecilia's Day concert of 1695 when nineteen amateur gentlemen musicians and eleven professional teachers of music met to play together. Many private concerts followed over the next ten years, but it was not until 1728 that the Musical Society

Access

Diversion down south side of the High Street via Niddry Street. See also Reid Concert Hall.

(Crown copyright: RCAHMS)

of Edinburgh was finally inaugurated at its regular meeting-place, the Cross Keys, Patrick Steill's tavern near Parliament Close.

In 1763 the new St Cecilia's Hall was completed (designed by the energetic royal master-builder Robert Mylne). In the foyer is a copy of the minutes of a meeting of the Directors of the Edinburgh Musical Society on 19 July 1759, at which Lord Provost George Drummond was elected Deputy Governor. Upstairs bronze busts of Raymond Russell and his mother survey part of the Russell Collection of Harpsichords and Clavichords. St Cecilia's Concert Hall is the oldest concert hall in Scotland and is said to have been based on the opera house at Parma in Italy. A contemporary description of 1779 comments: 'It is oval in form, the ceiling a concave elliptical dome, lighted solely from the top by a lanthorn. Its construction is excellently adapted for music; and the seats ranged in the room in the form of an amphitheatre are capable of containing a company of about five hundred persons.'

Perhaps the most colourful figure to have performed there was the Sienese castrato singer Giusto Ferdinando Tenducci, who shared the Tolbooth debtors' prison with the poet Robert Fergusson (who wrote a number of songs for him); in later years Tenducci sang for Mozart. Briefly married to an Irish girl, he was the only one of his kind to be recorded as having fathered a child.

Carrubber's Close

Access

No. 135, north side of the High Street.

Returning up to the north side of the High Street, we find Carrubber's Close. In 1450 it was the home of the merchant William Carrubber. It was later the home of Archbishop Spottiswood (1565–1639) of St Andrews, Lord Chancellor of Scotland, who in 1633 crowned Charles I at Holyrood.

From 1688 the close was a refuge for Jacobite sympathisers. When the Episcopalians were expelled from St Giles in 1689, Alexander Rose, Bishop of Edinburgh, founded Old St Paul's Church at the bottom of the close to house the congregation (which had at first worshipped in a nearby wool store). The Seabury Chapel in the close commemorates Bishop Samuel Seabury, the first bishop of the American Episcopal Church, who worshipped there while studying medicine at Edinburgh University and who was consecrated bishop there in 1784. Among the other members of the congregation were the song-writer Baroness Nairne, the poet William Aytoun and Scotland's greatest portrait painter, Sir Henry Raeburn. Allan Ramsay, who was a secret Jacobite sympathiser, opened a theatre in 1736 at Carrubber's Close. However, this was shut down in 1737 by the magistrates under the Licensing Act and the building reopened as the Whitfield Chapel. This in turn became 'the Celebrated Cathedral of the Prince of Darkness' when it was occupied by an atheist club in 1858. By May of that year it had been consecrated as the Carrubber's Close Mission, where Sir James Young Simpson was running a medical dispensary by 1865. The Whitfield Chapel in turn was demolished in 1872, and the foundation stone of the present Mission laid in 1883.

Bishop's Close

Bishop's Close was built by Thomas Sydeserf (1581–1663), Bishop of Brechin, then of Galloway and finally of Orkney. This was also the birthplace of Henry Dundas (later Lord Melville) in 1742. In the close lived the French Protestant Louis Cauvin, founder of the Cauvin Hospital for Boys at Duddingston. During the winter of 1786/7 Cauvin gave Robert Burns three French lessons a week at the Close. Cauvin himself is buried beside St Triduana's Chapel at Restalrig. His funds also went towards the construction of the Dean Orphanage (now the Dean Gallery of Modern Art).

Access

No. 129, north side of the High Street.

Access

South side of the High Street.

Blackfriars Street

Another brief diversion south takes us down Blackfriars Street, named after a monastery founded there in 1230 by King Alexander II. This was also the scene of the bloody street-fight in 1520 known as 'Cleanse the Causeway' between the Douglases and the Hamiltons. At the foot of the street was the palace of Cardinal David Beaton (1494–1546), who was also involved in the battle. Near his palace Walter Chepman and Andrew Myllar set up their press and in 1506 printed the first book in Scotland.

Access

No. 101, north side of the High Street.

Heave Awa' House

Heave Awa' House in Paisley's Close on the High Street was the site of a dramatic accident in 1861 when a tenement collapsed with the loss of thirty-five lives. While rescuers tore at the rubble they heard a voice shout 'Heave awa' chaps, I'm no' dead yet!' The survivor was a young boy, Joseph McIvor, who lived to a good old age. His portrait and the words of his cry are carved into the stone above the entrance to the close. Here also Sir William Fettes, wine and tea merchant and founder of Fettes College, once had his fashionable shop.

Trinity College Chapel

In Chalmers Close (no. 81 north) is all that remains of the once magnificent pre-Reformation Trinity College Church – just how magnificent can be seen from the Trinity College Altarpiece, a triptych on loan from Queen Elizabeth II to the National Gallery of Scotland at the Mound. The church was demolished in 1848 to make room for Waverley station, but part of it was reconstructed in 1872 off Jeffrey Street. Sadly, although carefully marked and stored on Calton Hill, many of the stones were stolen and the complete church could never be rebuilt.

The college was established in 1460 by Queen Mary of Gueldres (d. 1463), widow of James II, to provide divine worship with a provost and ten priests and to care for fourteen poor beadsmen (pensioners).

Access

North side of the High Street.

Whenever one of the priests said mass, he had to process in his vestments, carrying a hyssop plant, to the tomb of the founder and recite the *De profundis* ('Out of the depths. . .'). During the sixteenth century rich covers were placed on the altars, and there were also curtains with silk fringes around the head of the statue of the Virgin Mary. Silver chalices and reliquaries were used and services were enlivened by the music of organs and bells. The Dean of Trinity College had to be a doctor of laws, and, after the establishment of the Court of Session in 1532, was usually its president. During the years 1594–5 the Reformed communion service was celebrated at Trinity College. In 1594 the college accommodated the laureation (graduation) of Edinburgh University students in the presence of the queen and her ambassadors.

By 1726, however, the College Hospital had become dilapidated – slates were tumbling off the roof, threatening the lives of passers-by in the street below. The floor in the low gallery (the women's apartments) and its joists were all rotten. Through the north end of the house ran the waters of the Nor' Loch. In 1848 (before the college was finally dismantled to make way for the new North British Railway) a search was made for the body of the founder, Queen Mary of Gueldres. A skeleton was discovered and reburied in the royal vault at Holyrood on 15 July 1848. However, another skeleton was later uncovered near the high altar. The archaeologists believed this to be the queen. These remains were also buried in Holyrood Chapel, but *outside* the royal vault. Today Trinity College Apse is used as a popular brass-rubbing centre.

Hyndford's Close

Access

No. 34, south side of the High Street.

On the south side of the High Street is Hyndford's Close, formerly the mansion of the 3rd Earl of Hyndford (ambassador to a number of European courts during the War of the Austrian Succession, the Seven Years War and the Jacobite Rebellion). As a child, Jean Maxwell, Duchess of Gordon, fetched water from the well outside Fountain Close, riding on the back of a pig. In later years she became a friend of Robert Burns when he came to Edinburgh to enjoy its polite society. Professor Rutherford, the inventor of the gas lamp and grandfather of Sir Walter Scott, also lived there. In the nearby Lodge, St David, Scott himself became a Freemason.

Fountain Close

Each close provides a cross-section through several layers of history: in Fountain Close Thomas Bassendyne produced the first printed Bible in Scotland (1574). Between 1704 and 1781 the Royal College of Physicians had their premises in the close and opened a cold-water bath for the use of the public. The water-well which gave the close its name has now been moved across the High Street and down to the east. Today the Saltire Society for the promotion of Scottish language and culture is based there.

Access

No. 22, south side of the High Street.

Tweeddale Court

Tweeddale Court was built in 1576 for Dame Margaret Kerr, daughter of the 1st Earl of Lothian. Originally there was a garden there and an avenue of lime trees leading down to the Cowgate. The building was modernised by Robert Adam and two Doric columns added around 1799. Later it became the head office of the British Linen Bank, where in 1806 a bank messenger named William Begbie was murdered and robbed of £4,392: some of the money was recovered but the murderer was never found. In one corner of the court is a low stone shed with a sloping roof and slatted wooden doors: this is believed to be the last surviving sedan-chair store left in Edinburgh, a reminder of a once highly fashionable form of transport.

In 1817 the publishing firm of Oliver & Boyd took over the premises, remaining there until 1973. Today Tweeddale Court is the editorial home of *The List*, Edinburgh's (and Glasgow's) entertainment, events and lifestyle magazine.

Access

No. 14, south side of the High Street.

Museum of Childhood

The delightful Museum of Childhood exists today mainly because of the efforts of Councillor Patrick Murray (1908–81). Edinburgh-born and resident there all his life (apart from his schooldays at Stonyhurst in Lancashire), he was an optician before his election to the Town Council. While chairman of Edinburgh Corporation's Libraries and Museums Committee he started the Museum of Childhood, first in Lady Stair's

Access

At 42 High Street.

House in the Lawnmarket and, after eighteen months, in a new site on the High Street at Hyndford's Close. He began the collection with a number of his own childhood toys, 'a pitiful handful of soldiers, building blocks and railway stuff of my own'. The museum was the first of its kind in the world, dealing not just with toys, but with the customs, hobbies, health, upbringing and education of children from birth to around the age of twelve. Patrick Murray's bright idea, further developed in an accessible new building, has since been adopted in many other countries.

Moubray House

Access

North side of the High Street.

A private dwelling today, Moubray House is formed from a sixteenth-century addition to a fifteenth-century base. George Jamesone (1590–1644) the portrait painter had his studio on the upper floor. In 1706 the English journalist Daniel Defoe came to Edinburgh to spy for the government on the progress made towards the Union of the Parliaments and, as a cover, edited the *Edinburgh Courant*.

John Knox's House

Access

No. 45, south side of the High Street.

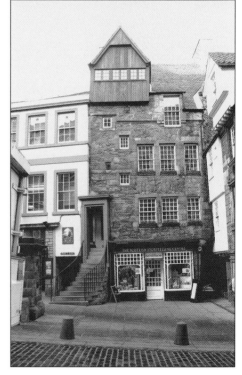

The Netherbow Arts Centre is an outreach initiative of the Church of Scotland. Currently (2005) it is undergoing a £3.4m refurbishment by the architectural firm of Malcolm Fraser, which will see the incorporation of a new Storytelling Court, an enlarged Netherbow Theatre and an upgraded John

Knox Museum, dedicated to the life of the influential Scottish Reformer and housed in a sixteenth-century house which was once more accurately the home of James Mosman, goldsmith to Mary, Queen of Scots, executed for treason in 1573.

(Copyright: F.C. Inglis)

World's End

The last close on the south side of the High Street is World's End Close, so called because it was next to the (now demolished) Netherbow Port (gate), which marked the boundary of the Old Town until the independent Burgh of Canongate became part of Edinburgh in 1856.

The World's End pub is still remembered today as the place where two 17-year-old girls were last seen alive in the company of two unidentified men in October 1977. Their bodies were later found in East Lothian: they had been raped and murdered. An active police investigation into the case is still (2005) ongoing.

Access

A public house on the corner of the High Street and St Mary's Street.

Netherbow Port

The location of the Netherbow Port (and the narrowness of the entry, only wide enough for a cart) can still be seen, marked out with brass plates set into the stone cobbles.

Access

Take care looking down at the brass markings, as traffic can be heavy at this busy junction.

Access

Immediately below the
Netherbow, a
continuation of the High
Street.

CANONGATE

Edinburgh owes its existence to the defensive advantages of the Castle Rock. The Royal Burgh of Canongate, on the other hand, was founded in 1143 by King David I for peaceful religious purposes and was built on the final section of the Royal Mile. The roles of the two burghs were complementary: the Sword and the Cross.

Until 1856 the Canongate was a distinct burgh, quite separate from the City of Edinburgh. In the nineteenth century it was a place of overcrowding and desti-tution. 'In Birtley Midcommon Close, Canongate,' recalled the surgeon Dr Alexander Wood in 1868, 'a modern tenement erected especially for dwellings for the poor, there are 35 rooms, 33 families, 24 children under five, 101 adults.' Attempts had already been made to alleviate the dire poverty in the area.

Making a short detour south into St Mary's Street, the visitor can see a plaque (above no. 2) which records that this was the first building erected under the Improvement Act of 1867 directed by Lord Provost William Chambers.

A little further down the road is Boyd's Entry, on the north wall of which another plaque commemorates the arrival at Boyd's Inn of Dr Samuel Johnson on 14 August 1773 during his Highland tour. It was here that Dr Johnson threw his glass out of the window.

Chessels Court and the Devious Deacon

Chessels Court, first built in around 1748, was the scene of the unmasking of Deacon William Brodie in 1787 when he was attempting

to rob the Excise Office there. Brodie had visited the office, taken impressions of the keys and memorised the layout of the building. The robbery took place on 5 March but all Brodie and his gang managed to steal was £16. Soon afterwards one of his accomplices turned king's evidence but Brodie managed to escape to the continent. He was eventually captured, tried in 1788 and executed at the west end of the Old Tolbooth (at the third attempt). His double life is said to have inspired Robert Louis Stevenson to write *Dr Jekyll and Mr Hyde*.

Morocco Land

The 'Moroccan' statuette high on the wall of Mid Common Close (no. 293) is said to commemorate a highly romantic tale. Young Andrew Gray, son of the Lord Provost's brother-in-law, was to be executed for helping to burn down the Lord Provost's house during the street violence which followed the coronation of Charles I in 1633. Sentenced to death, Gray managed to escape from the Tolbooth, reached Leith and escaped abroad by sea.

Some years later Edinburgh was ravaged by the plague. When the epidemic was at its worst an Algerian pirate ship was seen to anchor off Leith. Soon after this a strongly armed detachment of pirates arrived at the Netherbow Port and threatened to attack if a large ransom was not handed over. In reply the Provost gave his only daughter as security but pointed out that she was already ill with plague. The leader of the pirates promised to heal her. This he did in a house in the Canongate, and then he revealed himself as none other than Andrew Gray. He had fallen in love with the Provost's daughter and decided to spare the town the vengeance he had planned. The two were soon married and lived the remainder of their days in the Canongate. High on the wall above his house (273 Morocco Land) he placed a statue of his benefactor, the Emperor of Morocco (later moved to Mid Common Close).

The publisher and historian Robert Chambers has a different explanation: his version tells of a young Edinburgh woman who was kidnapped, taken abroad by an African slave-trader and sold to the Emperor of Morocco. From Morocco she wrote to her family, who arranged for her brother to trade between Africa and Edinburgh, so much so that his business prospered. In gratitude he erected a statue of the Emperor, wearing a turban and a necklace of precious stones.

The Canongate Playhouse

Access

No. 196, south side of the Canongate.

Old Playhouse Close once housed a flourishing theatre, the foundation stone of which was laid by John Ryan, a well-known Covent Garden actor. The theatre opened in 1747, putting Tailors' Hall, a rival establishment in the Cowgate, out of business. The first performance of the Revd John Home's tragedy *Douglas* took place there in 1756, its success inspiring the legendary shout from the audience of 'Whaur's yer Wullie Shakespeare noo?'

When the new Theatre Royal opened at the east end of Princes Street in 1769 the fortunes of the Old Playhouse rapidly declined. The poet Robert Fergusson (himself buried not far away in Canongate Kirkyard and now commemorated by a statue on the pavement outside the church) viewed the ruins of the theatre with regret:

No more, from box to box, the basket,
    piled
With oranges as radiant as the
    spheres,
Shall with their luscious virtues charm
    the sense
Of taste and smell. Oh! look here,
Upon this roofless and forgotten pile.

In front of Old Playhouse Close was St John's Cross, which was used for proclamations and other ceremonial events – such as the knighting of the Lord Provost by Charles I in 1633. Today it is commemorated by a large cross set inside a circle painted on the roadway.

Knights and Masons

On the south side of the Canongate in St John's Pend the Knights of the Order of St John had their houses, and today their priory is still on the same site.

The novelist Tobias Smollett (1721–71) stayed on the first floor in the Pend building with his sister Mrs Telfer in 1753, and again while writing *Humphrey Clinker* in the summer of 1766. The Canongate Kilwinning Lodge Hall (built in 1736 and thought to be the oldest Masonic lodge-room in the world) was visited by the poet Robert Burns in 1786. He was affiliated on 1 February and on 1 March 1787 the title of Poet Laureate was conferred on him.

Access

South side of the Canongate.

Access

No. 174, south side of
the Canongate.

Moray House

Moray House was built in about 1628 by the widow of the Count of
Home, an Englishwoman. Her initials 'M.H.' – Mary Home – can be
seen in various parts of the building. At her death the house passed to
her daughter Margaret, Countess of Moray. Both Charles I and the
Marquess of Argyll stayed in the house. In the summer of 1648 Oliver
Cromwell made Moray House his headquarters and it is said that while
there he revealed to the Covenanters his plan to execute Charles I. After
the Battle of Dunbar in 1650 Cromwell again spent some time there.

On 18 May 1650, soon after the wedding of the daughter of the 4th
Earl of Argyll, the chief guests are said to have assembled on the balcony
of Moray House to watch the Marquess of Montrose tied to a cart and
carried to the Parliament House to receive the death sentence. Montrose
was hanged at the Mercat Cross on 21 May. Only a year later the Earl of
Argyll suffered the same fate.

In 1753 Moray House was leased to the British Linen Company, who
filled it with staplers, spinners, weavers, packers and carters. In 1791–2 it
was occupied by Duncan Cowan, a paper-maker, but thereafter it
enjoyed a long and influential history as a college of education. Recently
Moray House became part of Edinburgh University.

(Crown copyright: RCAHMS (Chrystal Collection))

(By permission of Edinburgh University)

Moray House Pavilion

Completing the negotiations for the Treaty of Union between England and Scotland in 1707, the Scottish Lords signed the treaty in the small garden pavilion of Moray House (still there but in somewhat reduced splendour).

Shoemakers' Land

Shoemakers' Land once contained the Hall of the Incorporation of Cordiners (Shoemakers), built in 1682. In front of the building is a panel with the Cordiners' rounding or paring knife and the crown of St Crispin, accompanied by the observation that 'Blessed is he that wisely doth the poor man's case consider'.

Access

From Holyrood Road on the east side of Moray House. Today this is a service entrance.

Access

No. 197, north side of the Canongate.

Bible Land

Bible Land next door dates from 1677 and is so called from the two biblical quotations: 'Behold how good a thing it is and how becoming well together such as brethren are in unity to dwell' (Psalm 133) and 'It is an honour for a man to cease from strife' (Proverbs XX: 3).

Bakehouse Close

This close is well worth entering. Emerging from the pend (arched access way), the restored timber cladding and the contrasting textures of harling (Scottish pebble-dash), dressed stone (ashlar) and rubble walls give a good indication of the uninhibited variation in construction techniques over the centuries.

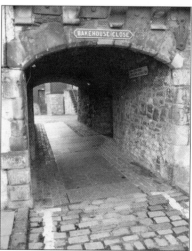

Museum of Edinburgh

The Museum of Edinburgh (formerly Huntly House Museum) examines the history of the city from earliest Roman times. Perhaps its most prized possession is a copy of the National Covenant. Other displays include Edinburgh silverware, the life of Field-Marshal Earl Haig, Greyfriars Bobby and shop signs.

(Copyright: F.C. Inglis)

Canongate Tolbooth

The Canongate Tolbooth (built in 1591 on the site of the Auld Tolbuith) had similar functions as Edinburgh's building of the same name. An inscription to James VI reads: 'Justice and Religion are a Ruler's strongest weapons.' The Canongate arms can also be seen: a stag's head with a cross caught in its antlers and the words 'This is the way to Paradise'.

Access

North side of the Canongate.

The People's Story Museum

The People's Story Museum inside the Canongate Tolbooth explores the lives of working people in Edinburgh from the 1780s to the 1980s. With sounds and smells and vivid reconstructions (such as a pub, a tea-room, a lodging-house booth and a wash-house), it brings the past vividly to life.

Access

No. 163, north side of the Canongate.

Acheson House

This was once the mansion of Sir Archibald Acheson of Abercairny (Secretary of State for Scotland in the time of Charles I) and of his wife Dame Margaret Hamilton. Sir Archibald became a Lord of Session in 1625, just after the accession of Charles I, and three years later bought one of the baronetcies of Nova Scotia (sasine to which was given with a piece of earth from the Castle Esplanade). The family crest of the Achesons can be seen from Bakehouse Close on the west side of the house: a cock standing on a trumpet with the motto 'Vigilantibus'. After

Access

South side of the Canongate.

a number of years variously occupied (including a period as a house of ill-repute, when the family motto was vulgarly referred to as 'The Cock and Strumpet'), Acheson House was restored in 1937.

Canongate Kirk and Graveyard

The Canongate Kirk was built in 1688 to accommodate the congregation of the Canongate after James VII ejected them from Holyrood (their traditional parish church) in order to convert the abbey church into a Roman Catholic chapel for the Knights of the Thistle. In 1745 Bonnie Prince Charlie's prisoners from the Battle of Prestonpans were held in the Canongate Kirk. In the grounds of the Kirk is the Canongate Mercat Cross, which stood from 1128 to 1888 just in front of what is now the main gate of the church. The octagonal shaft is sixteenth century and the capital and head date from 1888.

Among the celebrated figures buried in the churchyard are the ill-fated poet Robert Fergusson, George Drummond (six times Lord Provost

(By permission of City of Edinburgh Council)

and founder of the New Town), Professor James Gregory (inventor of the popular medicine 'Gregory's Mixture'), Agnes 'Nancy' Craig (Mrs Maclehose – the 'Clarinda' of Robert Burns' 'Sylvander'), the economist Adam Smith and the German musician Johann F. Lampe (Handel's favourite bassoonist).

(By permission of City of Edinburgh Council)

Canongate Golfer's Land

Golfer's Land was the home of John Paterson, whose grandfather had lived there from 1601. A plaque tells the story of the game of golf Paterson played with the Duke of York (later King James VII) in 1681 or 1682. The coat of arms above the plaque shows a hand gripping a golf-club over a helmet with the legend 'Far and Sure'. A notice refers to a

Latin inscription on the east-facing wall of the garden behind; said to have been written by Dr Archibald Pitcairne, it reads: 'When Paterson who, in succession to nine ancestors who had been champions, himself won the championship in the Scots' own game, he began to build up this house from the ground, which all alone produced so many champions.' Then follows the anagram of John Patersone: I hate no person.

Queensberry House

The house was built in 1682 by William, 1st Duke of Queensberry, who wielded enormous power in the reign of Charles II and was Lord High Commissioner early in the reign of James VII. He also helped to put William of Orange on the throne. The duke himself was a great miser but an extravagant builder of houses; although illiterate (he dictated all his letters to a secretary), paradoxically he was a great collector of books.

A horrific story is told about the son of the 2nd Duke of Queensberry, one of the principal architects of the Union of the Parliaments in 1707. His son, who had special educational needs but was extremely strong and very tall, was kept hidden away in a room at Queensberry House with boarded-up windows. On the day that the Treaty of Union was signed, the son's keeper left the room to watch the rioting crowds in the Canongate; when he returned he found to his horror the duke's son sitting in the kitchen roasting the kitchen-boy on a spit!

The 4th Duke of Queensberry and 3rd Earl of March (known as the 'Old Q') was a sporting man who spent much of his fortune on drink and entertainment. He sold Queensberry House to the government in 1801. In 1808 it was used as a barracks and then as a house of refuge for the destitute. Later it became a hospital and today is an integral part of the new Scottish Parliament complex.

Access

Brown's Close, No. 65, north side of the Canongate.

Access

No. 64, south side of the Canongate.

Queensberry House.

Access

North side of the
Canongate.

Scottish Parliament

The new Scottish Parliament, designed by the late Catalan architect
Enric Miralles, was officially opened by Her Majesty the Queen on
9 October 2004. After a ceremony at Parliament Hall (the home of the
Scottish Parliament until 1707), a historic Riding (procession) followed,
before the opening ceremony itself in the Debating Chamber. As the
new Scottish Parliament assembles in Edinburgh, it is worth recalling
the eloquent words of Andrew Fletcher of Saltoun, delivered in May
1703, warning of the dangers to Scotland of life without a Parliament:

If therefore either reason, honour, or conscience have any influence upon us; if we have any regard either to ourselves or posterity; if there be such a thing as virtue, happiness, or reputation in this world, or felicity in a future state, let me adjure you by all these, not to draw upon your heads everlasting infamy, attended with the eternal reproaches and anguish of an evil conscience, by making yourselves and your posterity miserable.

HOLYROODHOUSE

Legends and Beginnings

Holyrood Abbey (now a roofless shell) and the Palace of Holyroodhouse beside it both stand at the foot of the final section of the Royal Mile known as the Canongate. This religious and later royal complex began with King David I (*c.* 1080–1153) and his desire to improve Scotland.

Like Edinburgh Castle, the palace has a long cultural and political history. The colourful legend of the foundation of Holyrood is recorded in the *Holyrood Ordinale*, written in about 1450. The legend is based on the conversion of St Hubert (656–727), which in turn is copied from a second-century life of St Eustace, the patron saint of hunting. The founder of many Scottish monasteries, David loved hunting, so much so that he could not resist the chase even on holy days (when hunting was forbidden by the church). On 14 September 1128, the feast of the Exaltation of the Holy Rood (Cross), legend has it that David, going against the warnings of his confessor Alwyn, rode out into the Forest of Drumsheugh, which lay to the east below Edinburgh Castle, after hearing mass. He had just reached a small spring when suddenly he was confronted by a magnificent stag. David's horse reared up in fright and the king was thrown from his saddle. As he lay half-stunned on the ground he glanced up to see the sun's rays making the shape of a cross between the stag's antlers. David recovered from his fall but took this to be a stern reminder from God that he needed to mend his ways. The penance he and his confessor agreed on was that David should found a new monastery.

Access

The Palace of Holyroodhouse is a paid visitor attraction at the foot of the Royal Mile. Free parking is available for visitors to the palace or Holyrood Park at the eastern perimeter of the palace.

But the legend does not tell the full story. The king had other practical reasons for founding monasteries. They were an investment in the Scottish economy. As well as being powerhouses of prayer, they introduced modern methods of farming, improved crops and new breeds of cattle and horses as well as other industrial benefits; they brought literacy and social work to raise the quality of life of even the poorest man and woman.

David ordered the construction of the monastery of Holyrood (Holy Cross) close to the spring where he had had such a close encounter with death. Twenty skilled masons from France were sent for before the end of the year and the natural source at the scene of his hunting accident was henceforth known as 'The Spring of the Cross'. Then he brought Augustinian canons from Merton Priory in Surrey and gave them the right to erect a new burgh of Canongate (the canons' gait or walk). David made his confessor the first abbot.

From earliest times Holyrood was considered to be the most influential monastery in that part of Scotland, partly because its most treasured relic was the Black Rood of Scotland, said to be a fragment of the True Cross given by Queen Margaret to her husband King Malcolm Canmore. By 1250 Holyrood had administrative control of twenty-seven other local churches.

A second, much larger abbey was begun over the original church in the late twelfth century. By 1400 an imposing church with a nave of eight bays, north and south transepts, an aisled choir with a Lady Chapel, a chapter-house and soaring vaults in the roof (supported by flying buttresses) proclaimed the importance of the Augustinian canons and their work.

Over the coming centuries the abbey gave hospitality to the Kings of Scotland and it gradually became a favourite royal residence. The first mention of a 'royal chamber' comes in 1473, while in 1501 King James

(Copyright: F.C. Inglis)

IV began the construction of an exclusively royal residence of some size in preparation for his marriage (1503) to Margaret Tudor, daughter of Henry VII of England, which was celebrated by the poet William Dunbar in his poem 'The Thistle and the Rose' and was accompanied by jousting, feasting and dancing. The new palace was built over the outer court of the monastery and probably involved some adaptation of existing structures as well as fresh building.

Weddings and Funerals

David II was the first Scottish monarch to be buried at the abbey (1370), but it is with James II that Holyrood receives the seal of royal approval: he was born, crowned, married and buried (1460) there. Another royal celebration took place at Holyrood in 1469 when Margaret (*c.* 1457–86), daughter of Christian I of Denmark and Norway and wife of James III, was crowned Queen of Scotland.

The abbey was the scene of many of the marriages of Scotland's kings and queens: James II, James III, James IV, James V and Mary, Queen of Scots (to Lord Darnley). Burials in the royal vault included David II, James II and his queen, James V and his wife and Henry, Lord Darnley.

But construction was matched by destruction. In 1569 the east part of the abbey church was demolished by order of the General Assembly of the Church of Scotland (just as in 1688 a furious mob was to ransack the Catholic Chapel Royal and the Jesuit College established by James VII, breaking into the royal vault in the process). For the homecoming of James VI and I the palace was enthusiastically refurbished (as the wall paintings in Mary, Queen of Scots' bedroom indicate). When Charles I came to the abbey to be crowned in 1633 a similar redecoration took place. A less amicable welcome awaited him on his return in 1641, following his attempt to impose bishops on the Church of Scotland. Oliver Cromwell billeted his troops at Holyrood in 1651 and not long afterwards the royal apartments were damaged by fire. Cromwell,

however, was aware of the importance of the palace and rebuilding and extension took place in 1658–9.

It was with the Restoration that major rebuilding began: Charles II (who had been in Edinburgh in 1650) approved plans to rebuild the north, east and south sides of the main court, and the inscription marking the construction of a handsome piazza can still be seen today with the name of the master-mason, Robert Mylne, carved into the stone.

Sanctuary

The holy right of sanctuary at Holyrood derived from the foundation charter of David I. In earlier days the canons of Holyrood subjected aristocratic seekers after sanctuary to ordeal by fire (and the low-born to ordeal by water). In later times abuses crept in: criminals were admitted to sanctuary who should have suffered punishment in the civil courts. In 1532 the Scottish Court of Session came into being and shortly afterwards the Scottish Parliament passed an act compelling church sanctuaries to send offenders to the civil courts.

The boundaries of the royal sanctuary of Holyrood included the whole of the Royal Park from Salisbury Crags down to Duddingston Loch, the south of Abbeyhill, Dumbiedykes and even the crest of Arthur's Seat. Within this far-flung landscape lived the 'Abbey Lairds'. Future Lord Provost William Chambers (1800–83), while young, was a bookseller's apprentice appointed to sell lottery tickets to the inmates: 'The Sanctuary, which embraced a cluster of decayed buildings in front and on both sides of Holyrood Palace, was, at that time, seldom without distinguished characters from England – some of them gaunt, oldish gentlemen, seemingly broken-down men of fashion, wearing big gold spectacles, who now drew out existence here in defiance of creditors.' The old Girth Cross (now a traffic roundabout) was the visible symbol of sanctuary, located in the centre of the junction at the foot of the Canongate.

The 'Abbey Lairds' lived in cramped houses to the east of the palace. One observer described 'a variety of little miserable patchwork dwellings' from which the inmates anxiously scrutinised strangers. Every Saturday at midnight the Abbey Lairds could leave the sanctuary for 24 hours. On the stroke of midnight they streamed up the Canongate, some, like the writer Thomas De Quincey, to entertain the literati with their imaginative conversation, others on more worthy business, such as a minister who travelled as far as 20 miles to preach to his congregation. Some found the sanctuary gave them a breathing-space to work in: James Tytler (*c.* 1747–1805), for

example, composed large sections of the *Encyclopaedia Britannica* in the Debtors' Sanctuary and set up a press to print it. His manned hot-air balloon flight in 1784 (leading to his ignominious dive into a dung-heap) was made from the sanctuary of the Royal Park.

The most famous debtor at Holyrood was the Comte d'Artois, brother of Louis XVIII of France. He was installed in the palace from 1796 until 1803. After his abdication in 1831 he again returned to the sanctuary. His presence in the Canongate lent an air of raffish continental elegance to the burgh and 'Monsieur', as he was popularly known, aroused great affection by his charm and generosity as well as by his introduction of intriguing French foods and fashions.

Burnings, Rebuilding, Collapse and Reconstruction

In 1544 Holyrood Abbey had been burnt and looted by the Earl of Hertford, the English army returning three years later to strip the lead from the roof. The structure suffered further damage in the ensuing years. By 1570, in the Scottish Reformation period, Bishop Adam Bothwell, Commendator of Holyrood, was charged with negligence by the General Assembly for allowing the abbey to fall into disrepair.

Happier times came in 1633: Charles I decided to be crowned in the abbey and ordered its reconstruction. New windows were installed, and a tower built to house the enormous bells used to peal in celebration. A new west gable and door were also installed. Up to 1687 the abbey had been the parish church of the Canongate. In that year the parishioners were turned out of the abbey into the new Canongate Kirk and the abbey became a permanent Chapel Royal.

This improvement in the upkeep of the building was, however, relatively short-lived. In 1758 the decayed roof-timbers were removed and replaced by heavy stone slabs. In the course of the next ten years the weight of stone made the roof gradually collapse, bringing down other parts of the structure. So the romantic ruin visible today, open to the heavens, was finally formed and left scarred by the elements.

In spite of King George IV's triumphal visit to Edinburgh in 1822, Holyrood Abbey fell on hard times and became little more than a romantic ruin. In July 1829 the composer Felix Mendelssohn wrote: 'The chapel is now roofless, and is overgrown with grass and ivy, and the ruined Altar where Mary, Queen of Scots was married. Everything is in ruins and mouldering, and the bright light of Heaven shines in. I believe I have found the beginning of my Scottish Symphony there today.' In his notebook he had written down the Symphony's first sixteen bars.

Queen's Gallery

The Queen's Gallery facing the new Scottish Parliament is built in the shell of the former Holyrood Free Church and the Duchess of Gordon's School. The gallery was opened by Elizabeth II on 29 November 2002 as part of her Golden Jubilee celebrations. The new Gallery, designed by the Edinburgh architect Benjamin Tindall, is intended to display a varied programme of exhibitions drawn from the Royal Collection, especially works from the Royal Library at Windsor. The arched stone entrance is guarded by Scotland's heraldic lion; the arch itself has a carved garland of Scottish flowers. Downstairs, under the main exhibition gallery, computer screens give access to detailed catalogues of the Royal Collection.

Queen Mary's Bath-House

Access

Overlooking the pavement on the east side of the road at Abbeyhill.

The eccentric stone building known as 'Queen Mary's Bath-house' forces the road at Abbeyhill into an awkward bend. More probably a summer-house, it originally stood higgledy-piggledy in its idiosyncrasy, at the edge of the old Physic Garden; however, the construction of the north gate of the palace involved driving a roadway through the garden and so the 'Bath-house' was left high and dry, looking a little lost and sorry for itself, but clearly packed with hidden (but forgotten) history.

Our Dynamic Earth

Access

A paid visitor attraction.

Under a billowing roof white like a sail, visitors gather to chat and eat before being transported below to interactive exhibitions exploring the creation and development of the Earth – earthquakes shake the floor before the visitor moves through an ice age, while tropical forests offer entertainment for adults and children alike. The backdrop to the attraction is the red scarred face of Salisbury Crags, which gave the 'father of modern geology', James Hutton (1726–97), the material for his ground-breaking theory of the Earth's formation by volcanic activity.

Holyrood Park

Access

Entry is free for cars and pedestrians either through Duddingston Village, Holyrood Palace, Holyrood Park Road or from Meadowbank, with free car parking beside Holyroodhouse, at Duddingston Loch, at the Meadowbank entry and further up the circular but winding route to Dunsapie Loch and Arthur's Seat.

A royal park dedicated to the conservation of the environment, Holyrood Park still retains the aura of sanctuary. Depending on the sovereign, it is referred to as the 'Queen's Park' or the 'King's Park'. The nineteenth-century engineer James Nasmyth noted that 'When standing at the "Giant's Ribs" on the south side of Arthur's Seat, I felt as if one of the grandest pages of the Earth's history lay open before me.' Indeed, James Hutton used the rock formations at Salisbury Crags to demonstrate that volcanic activity was very significant in forming the landscape, although the prevailing popular belief was that it was shaped largely by the action of the sea in depositing layers of material. With its mighty volcanic hills, its crags and lochs and its stunning views of the city, the park provides a safe haven for walkers and sightseers. It offers a challenge to runners, and on 1 May each year is a place where the young can bathe their faces in the early morning dew in the hope of a rosy future. The park is one of the vital 'lungs' of the city and its benign influence touches many hearts. During his treatment at Craiglockhart for battle fatigue, the First World War poet Wilfred Owen wrote: 'I saw Holyrood on Sunday afternoon being alone on Salisbury Crags, a floating mirage in gold mist.'

SOUTHSIDE

Royal Infirmary

After 1870 the Royal Infirmary, Lauriston Place replaced William Adam's previous building in Drummond Street (1738). This placed the new hospital appropriately close to Edinburgh University's Medical School (1888), whose historic Anatomy Theatre can be visited by arrangement with the Department of Medicine. When the nineteenth-century building became too cramped and its location in the heart of the city too prone to grid-lock, it was succeeded in 2003 by a new and larger complex constructed to the south of Edinburgh at Little France. The former Royal Infirmary, Lauriston Place is currently being converted into a prestigious housing development.

Access

At Lauriston Place but the building is now being converted into commercial and residential accommodation.

George Heriot's School

The magnificent George Heriot's School was completed in about 1700, endowed by King James VI's banker and jeweller George Heriot as a school for destitute or orphaned children. Among its most famous pupils was the painter Sir Henry Raeburn, who came to the school as an orphan in 1764. The gardens of the school were used as a launch-pad in 1787 by the Italian balloonist and highly romantic self-publicist Vicenzo Lunardi, while the Defensive Bands of Edinburgh trained there during the Napoleonic Wars. Today Heriot's, a private fee-paying school, has an enviable reputation for academic excellence.

Access

At Lauriston Place – the exterior of the school can be viewed by the public using discretion and with permission, mindful of child protection issues – ask permission at the school office and visit outside school hours.

(By permission of George Heriot's School)

National Museums of Scotland

Access

Halfway along
Chambers Street; entry
is free but for special
exhibitions an entry fee
may be charged.

The foundation stone of the Royal Museum of Scotland was laid by
Prince Albert in 1861, only two months before his death. It was built by
a military engineer and is a comprehensive museum built around
Edinburgh University's Natural History Museum, and incorporates a
new Industrial Museum.

Today the museum is particularly child-friendly, full of exotic animals
and fascinating mechanical exhibits. To the west is the new Museum of
Scotland (1998), an exciting space built to interpret the richness and
variety of Scottish history. The restaurant on the roof and the café on
the ground floor are both worth patronising.

Greyfriars Kirk

Access

From Candlemaker Row
and George IV Bridge.
Entry to the graveyard
and church is free but
visitors should respect
the needs of a working
church.

The land at Greyfriars was formerly the home of Franciscan priests who
came to Edinburgh in 1447 as medical missionaries to tend the poor and
sick. In 1562, after the Reformation, the Franciscans fled to the
continent. Their garden was later given to the town by Mary, Queen of
Scots as an overflow cemetery
to relieve the overcrowding in
the churchyard of St Giles,
the parish church of Edinburgh. Greyfriars Kirk itself
was built after the Reformation; there the momentous
National Covenant was
signed in 1638 as a protest at
the English style of worship
which had recently been
imposed on the Scots.

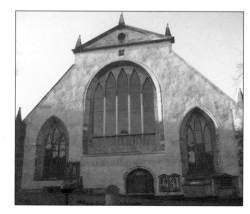

(By permission of City of Edinburgh Council)

Many of the most illustrious of Edinburgh's men and women are buried in the churchyard, including the poet Allan Ramsay (1686–1758), the Latin scholar and hanging judge Sir George Mackenzie (1636–91), James Hutton (1726–97), the 'father of modern geology', the chemist Joseph Black (1728–99), discoverer of latent heat, and the extraordinary judge and anthropologist James Burnett, Lord Monboddo (1714–99). Between 1562 and 1900 nearly 100,000 people were buried in the churchyard, even changing the composition of the soil. 'Greyfriars is continually overrun by cats,' wrote Robert Louis Stevenson. 'I have seen, one wintry afternoon, as many as thirteen of them seated on the grass beside old Milne, the Master Builder, all sleek and fat and complacently blinking, as if they had fed upon strange meats.'

Edinburgh University

Access

From Chambers Street or the South Bridge. The Talbot Rice Gallery in the Old Quad is worth a visit.

Edinburgh University was the first post-Reformation university in Scotland and was founded not by the Church but by the Town Council. It was first known as 'the Tounis College' but in 1617 achieved the status of 'King James' University'. The first regent (principal) in 1583 was Robert Rollock, a 28-year-old scholar from Stirling. Students were aged between 16 and 19 at that time, and graduates of the university have from time immemorial been capped with 'the Seat of Learning' in the shape of 'Geordie Buchanan's breeks', the original trousers of the Reformation scholar and teacher George Buchanan, who is buried in Greyfriars kirkyard.

The university can boast a number of Nobel prizewinners, among them Professor Charles Glover Barkla (Professor of Natural Philosophy 1913–22) and the former principal Sir Edward Appleton. Their awards were made for work in revealing the nature of X-radiation and in physics respectively. In politics the university has also been influential. Prime Ministers Palmerston and Russell were educated mainly in Edinburgh. Sir Alfred Ewing, principal of the university, enabled the United States to decipher the notorious Zimmerman telegram in which the German Foreign Secretary encouraged Mexico to attack the USA in 1917, infuriating American opinion and speeding up the USA's entry into the First World War.

The exterior of the Old Quad is by Robert Adam (1789), and the interior by William Playfair. The large and imposing dome topped by the 'Golden Boy' carrying the Torch of Learning is by the architect Sir Robert Rowand Anderson. From 1825 to 1827 Charles Darwin

(By permission of Edinburgh University)

(1809–82) and his brother Erasmus were students at the university and lodged on the fourth floor of the now demolished 11 Lothian Street (commemorated by a plaque inside the Royal Museum, Chambers Street). Among the most unusual graduates was Dr James Miranda Stuart Barry (1799–1865) who began to study medicine at the university at the age of 10, at a time when women were officially excluded from medical schools. Barry went on to become Inspector-General of Military Hospitals in Canada but, upon his deathbed, was found to have been a woman.

Edinburgh Festival Theatre

Access

Nos 13–29 Nicolson Street.

Today one of Edinburgh's leading venues, the Festival Theatre was the result of many years of ignominious wrangling between opera lovers and the city authorities over the infamous 'hole in the ground', an embarrassing gap-site from 1965 to 1991 below the castle, a notorious symbol of civic dithering and lack of confidence in the arts. With its daring glass façade and its broad range of entertainment, the Festival Theatre however has bridged the gap between so-called 'elite' and popular arts.

Originally known as the Empire Theatre (1929), the building saw one of the most intriguing of Edinburgh's many bizarre historical episodes. In the spring of 1911 the 38-year-old Californian Sigmund Neuberger, a friend of Houdini and a master of disguise and theatrical effects (known professionally as 'the Great Lafayette'), was killed when fire broke out at the climax of one of his most daring illusions. In 'The Lion's Bride' a beautiful woman was about to be torn apart by a lion but was saved at the very last moment by Lafayette (who, dressed as a lion, took the place of the real animal).

An electric wire fused on stage during the performance and the scenery was quickly ablaze. The audience managed to get out unharmed but seven badly burned bodies were found on the stage. Neuberger was buried after a public procession through the city (which still exists on film). Then, some days later, it became apparent that it was not his body they had buried, but that of his stage-double. In the end the Great Lafayette was buried in Piershill Cemetery (near Portobello), in the grave in which his beloved performing dog, Beauty, had been interred not long before.

Surgeons' Hall

Access

The main entrance is on Nicolson Street; entrance to the museum is behind at 9 Hill Square.

Designed by William Playfair, the Surgeons' Hall (1832) was built to accommodate the Royal College of Surgeons founded in 1505 by James IV from the Guild of Barber-Surgeons. From 1826 to 1831 Dr Robert

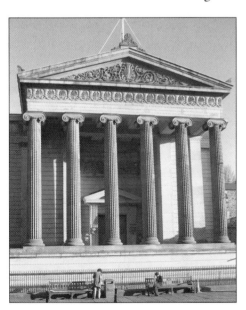

Knox was conservator of the College's Museum and provided a very popular and successful course of lectures in anatomy, as well as incurring notoriety for his involvement with the body-snatchers Burke and Hare, who supplied corpses for anatomical dissection. A fascinating free-entry History of Surgery museum is open to the public and the magnificent Surgeons' Hall itself, with portraits by Sir John Medina, can also be seen by arrangement with the college.

John Forbes Automotive

Access

No. 7 Meadow Lane.

Born in 1932, John Forbes, an American Korean War veteran from San Diego, presides over his garage, tucked away down Meadow Lane, next to Archers' Hall, home of the Royal Company of Archers, the Queen's Bodyguard for Scotland.

Forbes is a tall gentle man, with a white beard that would not disgrace an Old Testament prophet. A green VW Beetle, sliced in half, is fixed high up on the red stone wall outside his garage where he coaxes elderly and not-so-elderly VW Beetles back to life – a surreal symbol for the man himself who spent fifteen years bush-flying and dredging rivers for gold and diamonds in British Guiana, before meeting his Glasgow-born wife who had come, he says, 'looking for wild animals and found me!'

Forbes's grandfather was born in Aberdeen but spent his life home-steading in Nebraska, USA. His father later moved south to California. In 1960 Forbes was bitten by the VW Beetle bug and was tempted to reform his hard-living ways but, as one of the jockey-caps sitting on his desk records, 'I gave up sex, smoking and drinking. It was the worst 20 minutes of my life.'

Access

A private residence at
64 St Leonard's Street.

Hermits and Termits

Standing in front of the obelisk-like Waterloo Well is the former stationmaster's office, Hermits and Termits. Built in 1734 and restored in 1918, the house gate is made of elegant floral ironwork, while the crest above the house door shows a blue swan over a coronet. At one time the house belonged to Robert Scott, an engraver. His two sons William (1811–90), a pre-Raphaelite painter, and David (1806–49), a painter of imaginative scenes from history, grew up in the house. David, who suffered from a psychiatric illness, is buried in the Dean Cemetery.

NEW TOWN

FIRST NEW TOWN

Proposals for enlarging Edinburgh by the construction of a New Town to the north were first published in 1752. The scheme owed much to George Drummond, Lord Provost of Edinburgh from 1750 to 1751 (his third term in office). This plan was made necessary by the very serious overcrowding of the Old Town and the dangerous state of some of the buildings which had resulted in several tenements collapsing with tragic consequences. The major constructions involved in building the New Town were the draining of the man-made Nor' [north] Loch (1759), the construction of the North Bridge (1772) and the building of Register House (1774).

The plan of the New Town finally chosen in 1776 was that of the young architect James Craig. His idea was to build on a geometrical gridiron pattern which, many years later, Hans Christian Andersen, then visiting the city, thought had been inspired by Scottish tartan! The poet Robert Burns described the regularity of the New Town somewhat sardonically as 'heavenly Hanoverianism' but to the judge Henry, Lord Cockburn, commenting in 1822, the year of King George IV's visit to Edinburgh, the early New Town was a place of delight:

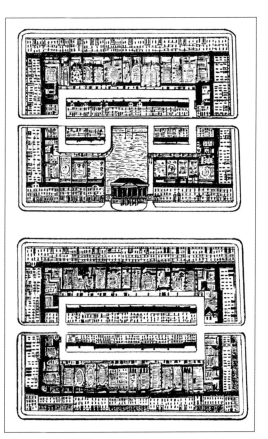

> It was then an open field of as green turf as Scotland could boast of, with a few respectable trees on the flat, and thickly wooded on the bank along the Water of Leith . . . how can I forget the glory of that scene on the still nights on which I have stood in Queen Street, or the opening of the north-west corner of Charlotte Square, and listened to the ceaseless rural corn-craiks nestling happily in the dewy grass.

Princes Street Publishers

James Grant (1883) records the comical way in which Princes Street received its name. The new road was originally to be named St Giles Street, but King George III refused to allow this, as St Giles was also the name of a seedy district in London:

> The first thoroughfare, now a magnificent terrace, was called St. Giles Street, after the ancient patron of the city; but on the plan being shown to George III for his approval, he exclaimed, 'Hey, hey! – what, what! – St. Giles Street! – never do, never do!' and so, to escape from a vulgar London association of ideas, it was named Princes Street, after the future Duke of York.

The south-facing fronts of Princes Street have so completely changed since the eighteenth century that little trace of the originals remains. In the first block between West Register Street and South St Andrew Street were once the premises of the most influential publishers in Britain: Archibald Constable at no. 10 and seven doors along William Blackwood at no. 17. Constable's shop, which he set up in 1822, saw the birth of a new dimension in publishing.

Constable had first begun work as a lad in the bookshop of Peter Hill at Parliament Close. Hill had acted for Robert Burns in commercial matters as he was City Treasurer and a governor of Heriot's Hospital. In 1795 Constable set up on his own at the north side of the High Street as

(Copyright: F.C. Inglis)

a bookseller and publisher. In 1801 he took over the *Scots Magazine* and in 1802 published the first number of the *Edinburgh Review*. He then bought over the copyright and stock of the *Encyclopaedia Britannica* in 1812. Constable, whose business style was characterised by inflated prices along with extraordinary generosity, then began an association with Sir Walter Scott, publishing his novels. Unhappily, in 1826 financial disaster struck which wore down even Constable's enormous optimism and giant frame. He died in 1827, soon dragging Scott with him into financial ruin.

Duke of Wellington Statue

Access

East end of Princes Street, in front of Register House.

The first of the metal castings for the equestrian statue of the duke by Sir John Steell took place at the end of May 1849 at a foundry specially built for the job in Grove Street. Early on a mid-June morning the enormous statue (which weighed 12 tons) was towed by 30 men and 8 horses to its site in front of Register House at the east end of Princes Street. The bronze glittered brightly in the sun for the public unveiling on 18 June 1852, the anniversary of the Battle of Waterloo. A public holiday had been declared and the city was packed with curious onlookers. The 79th Highlanders stood in single file along the North Bridge, their plumes visible above the heads of the crowd. The 7th Hussars were placed at intervals along Princes Street, the North and South Bridges and Waterloo Place. Every roof was covered with people perched on platforms. A large Masonic procession passed from the university to Register House, led by the Duke of Buccleuch, who made a speech on the life of Wellington. Then the statue was unveiled to the applause of the crowds and the accompaniment of the military bands who played 'See the Conquering Hero Comes'; the deafening firing of the guns at the castle was answered by a battery on the crest of Salisbury Crags. That evening, however, the weather changed dramatically and those who attended a second ceremony had to endure a violent thunderstorm, giving rise to the following verse:

Mid lightning's flash and thunder's
    echoing peal,
Behold the Iron Duke, in bronze,
    by Steell!

Access

At the east end of Princes Street. Entry is free but the extraction of some records may be chargeable.

General Register House

Robert Adam's Register House (1774–1822), formerly the Scottish Record Office, was built to house the national archives of Scotland. The Historical Search Room contains a wealth of local and national records such as parish or kirk session records.

Behind it is New Register House (1863), which holds the registration records of births, marriages and deaths (registration having become compulsory in 1855). Other records are held at West Register House in Charlotte Square, including government archives.

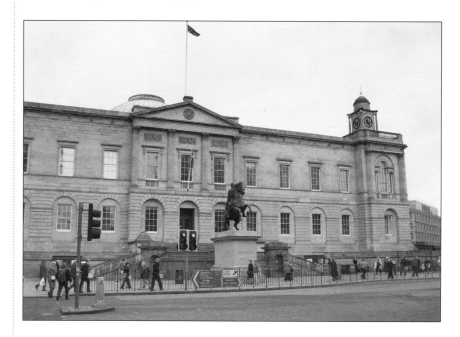

Access

From the top of Waterloo Place (on foot) or from Regent Road (by car).

Calton Hill

In the nineteenth century Calton Hill was used to dry linen sheets; more recently it is the location for the Beltane Fire Festival held every year during the night of 30 April.

Access

Beside the steps from Waterloo Place.

Scottish Singers

Calton Hill enjoys a unique location overlooking the east end of Princes Street. Up the steps at the eastern top of Waterloo Place, there is a large plaque on the right to three famous Scottish singers: the Covent Garden tenor John Wilson (1800–49), the Drury Lane operatic tenor John Templeton

(1802–86) and the baritone David Kennedy (1825–86), father of the folk-song collector Marjory Kennedy-Fraser and an ancestor of the contemporary violinist Nigel Kennedy. To the left is Rock House, a private residence where the photographic pioneers David Octavius Hill (1802–70) and Robert Adamson (1821–48) made their early 'sun-pictures'.

Nelson Monument

Note: People with a heart condition should not attempt to climb the monument.

At the top of the steps (uncannily reminiscent of the approach to the Acropolis in Athens) the 106-foot high Nelson Monument towers above the city from its base 456 feet above sea-level. Designed by Robert Burn in 1807 in imitation of an upturned telescope, the view-point from its 143 steps is stunning but usually extremely windy. The monument commemorates Admiral Horatio Nelson's victory at the Battle of Trafalgar off Cape Trafalgar in south-west Spain on 21 October 1805. The time-ball on top of the tower was designed to drop simultaneously with the firing of the One o'Clock Gun at Edinburgh Castle as a signal to shipping in the River Forth.

National Monument

Only the base and a number of columns are still in place.

Beyond Nelson's Monument stands the National Monument, which was intended to be a memorial to the fallen of the Napoleonic Wars. George IV laid the foundation stone in 1822 in what was meant to be the Hall of Heroes but the project was undersubscribed and never completed: only half of the £42,000 needed was raised – hence the nickname 'Edinburgh's Folly' or 'Edinburgh's Disgrace'.

City Observatory

At the centre of Calton Hill are the City Observatories: the Old (designed by James Craig in Gothic style and completed in 1792) and William Playfair's domed New Observatory (1818). Edinburgh's working observatory, the Royal Observatory, is now located south of the city at Blackford Hill.

Dugald Stewart's Monument

The varied architecture of Calton Hill is graced by Playfair's graceful monument to the philosopher Dugald Stewart (1753–1828), whose body lies far below in the Canongate kirkyard, obscured by an overgrowth of ivy.

Old Calton Burial Ground

Below Calton Hill is the Old Calton Graveyard which once stretched across what is now Waterloo Place; headstones can still be seen on the other side of the road. Among the many illustrious and fascinating people buried in the Old Calton are 'Indian Peter' Williamson (1730–99), who was press-ganged from the harbour in Aberdeen and sold into slavery in Philadelphia. Scalped by Indians, he escaped and retired to Edinburgh where he opened a tavern and organised the first penny post and street directory in Edinburgh (1773). To the left the towering black obelisk of the Martyrs' Monument commemorates the five men who fought for electoral reform and were sent to Botany Bay in Australia for their trouble. Among them was the lawyer Thomas Muir (1765–98), whose words to the hanging judge Lord Braxfield still echo down the years: 'When our ashes shall be scattered by the winds of heaven, the impartial voice of future times will rejudge your verdict.'

To the right are monuments to the philosopher David Hume (1711–76) and to Abraham Lincoln's freeing of the slaves (said to be the first such statue in Europe), together with the graves of five Scotsmen who died fighting in the American Civil War.

Access

On the south side of Waterloo Place. It is important, when visiting any Edinburgh graveyard, to take a friend. Some of the city graveyards present formidable obstacles such as 15-foot high giant hogweed, or danger from the only too real human spectres lurking in the ruins of long-forgotten tombs. For safety's sake do not walk alone!

(By permission of City of Edinburgh Council)

(By permission of City of Edinburgh Council)

Walking carefully through the graveyard, turn left round the back of the barrel-shaped David Hume monument to reach the highly ornamented black gate to the last resting-place of publisher William Blackwood (1776–1834). *Blackwood's Magazine* was launched under its editor Blackwood, who was himself born in Edinburgh in very humble circumstances and was first apprenticed at Bell & Bradfute in Parliament Close. Having spent some time in Glasgow and London he then returned to Edinburgh and set up in business on the South Bridge as a dealer in antiquarian books. In 1810 he helped to found the *Edinburgh Encyclopaedia*.

In 1816 Blackwood moved to Princes Street to premises frequented by Tory literary men. As in his future establishment at 45 George Street, his Princes Street business was laid out in an enticing series of compartments which drew the visitor into the heart of the building – 'an elegant oval saloon, lighted from the roof, where various groups of loungers and literary dilettanti are engaged in looking at, or criticising among themselves, the publications just arrived by that day's coach from town,' noted J. G. Lockhart. Beyond Blackwood's grave, hidden under the immense ivy on the wall, is the grave of another great publisher, Archibald Constable (1774–1827), the demise of whose business in 1826 bankrupted Constable himself and brought on his early death, and also ruined Sir Walter Scott.

Burns Monument

Access

Regent Road (south side).

Overlooking the New Calton Cemetery, the Robert Burns Monument by Thomas Hamilton (1830) is a variation on his earlier monument to the poet at Alloway in Ayrshire (1820). Originally the Edinburgh Burns Monument contained within its base the fine marble statue of the poet by John Flaxman (1755–1826), which is now to be found in the entrance hall of the Scottish National Portrait Gallery in Queen Street.

St David Street – Scott and Hume

Access

From the east end of Princes Street or St Andrew Square.

After the death of his wife and the breaking-up of his home in North Castle Street, Sir Walter Scott lived at 6 North St David Street from March to July 1826, lodging with a Mrs Brown. Although Scott was in mourning, he had his butler from Abbotsford in attendance.

For the last part of his life the home of the philosopher and historian David Hume (1711–76) was at 21 South St David Street. James Nasmyth (the inventor of the steam-hammer) in his *Autobiography* wrote: 'My grandfather built the first house in the south-west corner of St Andrew Square, for the occupation of David Hume the historian, as well as the two most important houses in the centre of the north side of the same square.'

On the wall of this house occurred the humorous incident which gave the street its curious name. Wanting to poke fun at the strongly agnostic Hume who, although a kind and generous friend, disbelieved in the existence of God, some of his acquaintances wrote 'SAINT DAVID STREET' on his wall. Seeing it in the morning, Hume's young maid ran in to tell her master, expecting an explosion of indignation. Instead, Hume saw the funny side of the graffiti and all ended happily with the facetious title being cheerfully adopted by the people of Edinburgh.

Scott Monument

Access

A paid attraction overlooking Princes Street at East Princes Street Gardens.

On 15 August 1840 (the anniversary of the birth of Sir Walter Scott) the foundation stone of the monument was officially laid. The day had been declared a public holiday. The Lord Provost and many dignitaries processed, accompanied by armed dragoons. The end of the ceremony was marked by a seven-gun salvo from a battery on the opposite slope of Princes Street Gardens.

However, tragedy marred the subsequent construction. The monument's architect, George Meikle Kemp, returning from a visit to a building contractor at the side of the Union Canal in Fountainbridge, apparently slipped in the fog, fell into the canal and was drowned. His body was only discovered a week later. Kemp is buried in St Cuthbert's Cemetery, at the corner of Princes Street and Lothian Road. There were

(Copyright: F.C. Inglis)

some who suspected foul play on the part of other disgruntled and unsuccessful candidates in the competition to design the monument, but nothing could be proved.

People's opinions of the monument were not all favourable: Charles Dickens, a frequent visitor to Edinburgh, disliked it: 'I am sorry to report the Scott Monument a failure. It is like the spire of a Gothic church taken off and stuck in the ground.' John Ruskin, the artist and historian, thought it should have been placed on Salisbury Crags and dismissed it as a 'small vulgar Gothic steeple'.

St Andrew Square – Lord Brougham and Sir Walter Scott

Access

No. 21 at the north-west corner of St Andrew Square.

Henry, Lord Brougham (1778–1868), born at no. 21, was educated at the High School; he became an advocate in 1800, being admitted to the English bar eight years later. An MP by 1810, he also served as Lord Chancellor (1830–4). Brougham was one of the founders of the *Edinburgh Review* and popularised the carriage called after him – the brougham. He also helped to found the Academy of Physics at Edinburgh (1797). In 1859 Brougham Place was named after him.

On the east side of the square (nos 34–5) is a building once known as the Douglas Hotel. Here in 1832 Sir Walter Scott spent his last two nights in Edinburgh.

St Andrew Square – Dundas, Hopetoun and Melville

Access

On the east side of St
Andrew Square. It is a
working bank, so access
is free and photographs
can be taken with
permission.

Immediately next door is the registered head office and flagship bank of
the Royal Bank of Scotland, designed by Sir William Chambers (1771)
for Sir Laurence Dundas. In 1794 it became the Excise Office and in
1825 was acquired by the Royal Bank. In the vestibule of the bank is a
bronze plaque set into the floor showing the original surveyor's setting-
out point for the New Town plan.

The roof of the telling-hall is covered by an extraordinary dark blue
ceiling through which daylight is filtered through dazzling concentric
circles of stars. On the grass in front of the bank stands the bronze
Hopetoun Monument (1834) by Thomas Campbell which shows John,
4th Earl of Hopetoun (1765–1823), governor of the bank from 1820 to
1823, standing in the costume of a Roman general beside his obedient
horse. A professional soldier, he served in the West Indies and
commanded the left flank of the British army at Corunna. He was also
an MP and Captain of the Royal Archers.

In the centre of St Andrew Square is the Melville Monument,
surmounted by a 14-foot high statue of Edinburgh-born Henry Dundas
(1742–1811), 1st Viscount Melville, Solicitor-General for Scotland, MP
for Edinburgh, holder of a number of key government posts under
William Pitt the Younger. Dundas eventually gained complete control
over the electoral system in Scotland and was known as 'the absolute
dictator of Scotland' or 'Harry the Ninth, uncrowned King of Scotland'.

York Place – Sir Henry Raeburn

North-east of St Andrew Square is York Place where, at no. 32, Sir Henry Raeburn (1756–1823) built himself a house in 1795; the top floor was lit by skylights to provide space for exhibiting portraits, while the lower floors were fitted out as the painter's studios. Raeburn's iconic painting, *Revd Dr Robert Walker skating on Duddingston Loch* (*c.* 1795), is believed to have inspired the design of the MSPs' irregularly shaped 'think pods' at the Scottish Parliament building.

York Place – The Nasmyths

Alexander Nasmyth (1758–1840), painter and engineer, trained as an artist with Allan Ramsay and later went to Italy where he specialised in painting landscapes and buildings. His most famous (and probably most authentic) portrait was that of Robert Burns, which he worked on in the poet's lodgings in the Lawnmarket. Nasmyth also collaborated with Patrick Miller of Dalswinton in designing and testing a steamboat. One of his sons was the landscape painter Patrick Nasmyth (1787–1831), while another, James Nasmyth (1808–90), was a celebrated engineer, inventor of the steam-hammer and many other innovations. The impressive Nasmyth family tomb is in the Dean Cemetery and bears a carving of the family crest, a broken hammer ('nae smith' – no smith).

(By permission of the Dean Cemetery Trust)

EASTERN NEW TOWN

Picardy Place – Sir Arthur Conan Doyle

Access

At the top of Leith Walk, beside the first roundabout at Picardy Place.

Sir Arthur Conan Doyle (1859–1930), doctor and novelist, was born at 11 Picardy Place, in a house which no longer exists. His father, an assistant surveyor at the Scottish Office, was a skilful caricaturist, and two of his paintings are in the City Art Centre's collection.

Conan Doyle himself studied medicine at Edinburgh University, living in George Square, and was a keen sportsman who later played cricket for the MCC. His greatest achievement was the creation of Sherlock Holmes, the masterly detective who lived at 221B Baker Street with his assistant Dr Watson. Holmes was modelled on Dr Joseph Bell (buried in Edinburgh's Dean Cemetery), one of Conan Doyle's lecturers, and Dr Watson on the surgeon Sir Patrick Heron-Watson. The house at 11 Picardy Place was demolished some years ago but today a quizzical statue of the great detective stands guard over the spot where his creator was born.

Baxter's Place nos 1–8 – Robert Stevenson House

Access

Top of Leith Walk, on the east side, just below the Playhouse Theatre.

This restored property was once the office of the Stevenson family's engineering firm founded by Robert Louis Stevenson's grandfather Robert (1772–1850). His stepfather was the designer of a reflector light adopted by the Northern Lighthouse Board in 1780 as a standard for Scotland's first four lighthouses. Stevenson became his stepfather's assistant in 1790 and built his first lighthouse at Portpatrick in 1792. By 1797 he was in complete control of the business. Stevenson and his workmen spent two construction seasons living in cramped and dangerous conditions on the Bell Rock on the Inchcape. Soon he was appointed sole engineer to the Lighthouse Commissioners (one of whom was Sir Walter Scott).

Robert Stevenson made many notable contributions to the development of the City of Edinburgh: he extended Princes Street

beyond the East End and round the base of the Calton Hill, supervising the construction of Regent Road. He produced the plan for the Calton Gaol (on the site of the present St Andrew's House), planned the drainage of what was to become Princes Street Gardens, designed the first railway line to Edinburgh and directed the building of access roads on many sides of the city.

Stevenson had three sons, all of whom followed him into the civil engineering profession in the family firm, and all became engineers to the Northern Lighthouse Board.

Access

At the top of Leith Walk in front of the steps of St Mary's Cathedral, Picardy Place.

Manuscript of Monte Cassino Sculpture

Outside St Mary's Cathedral at the top of Leith Walk stands the *Manuscript of Monte Cassino* (see title page), Leith-born sculptor Sir Eduardo Paolozzi's (1924–2005) best-known piece of work in Edinburgh. The work recalls both the area from which most of Edinburgh's Italians came and the ferocious and destructive Second World War battle over the Benedictine abbey there. Paolozzi himself had been briefly interned before studying at Edinburgh College of Art.

Using fragments of a human form (a giant hand, a foot – see title page – and an eye-ball), Paolozzi aimed to create a haven of peacefulness in the face of one of the city's most heavily used roundabouts. The sculpture also incorporates Latin inscriptions taken from a poem written by an exiled Italian monk 1,200 years ago, and discarded stones from the old Leith Central station (close to where he lived as a child and helped in his parents' Leith café). The whole work not only provides a talking-piece for adults but also offers a dramatic and humorous slide (the giant foot) for children.

It is entirely fitting that the city has housed Paolozzi's studio and its working materials in a new Dean Gallery at Belford Road (formerly the Dean Orphanage, founded by Louis Cauvin, the teacher to whom Robert Burns went for French lessons three times a week during the winter of 1786–7, and who is buried at Restalrig beside St Triduana's Well).

Elm Row Pigeons

Larger than life five imperious 20lb bronze pigeons strut on the pavement, rubbing shoulders with the unconcerned real-life birds of the capital, chasing tit-bits. The whimsical work of sculptor Shona Kinloch for the Turnbull Jeffrey Partnership, the birds lend an air of pacific calm to the frenetic and noisy life of the street. Despite being commended by the Civic Trust, the birds have been in the wars: one of the original seven birds has disappeared altogether (probably dispatched by a reversing lorry), while only the imprint remains of another.

Access

Just north of the roundabout at the top of Leith Walk.

Valvona & Crolla

At the head of Leith Walk stands the unpretentious façade of the Italian delicatessen and produce shop, Valvona & Crolla, still with the windows boarded up as they had been during the Second World War when Italian businesses were targeted by vandals who threw bricks at their windows.

Inside, the shop was a tiny corner of provincial Italy, an Aladdin's Cave of what the Edinburgh-based winner of TV's Master Chef competition, Sue Lawrence, once described as 'hillocks of aged parmesan, long knobbly salami and fabulous bottles of glistening olive oil'. But it was the 'in your face' bonhomie of Victor Contini which gave Valvona & Crolla its special atmosphere. He would greet every surprised stranger who sidled shyly into the shop as if he or she were one of the family.

Today, the Contini family at Valvona & Crolla has updated the shop and diversified logically enough into the wine and restaurant business, opening other premises at Multrees Walk off St Andrew Square and in George Street. From time to time (especially during the Festival) the new light and airy Caffè Bar at the back of the old Elm Row shop opens an intimate auditorium for music or theatre, entertainments often enhanced with the songs of Italy sung by Philip Contini or with those of his theatrical colleague, Edinburgh musician Mike Maran.

Access

Elm Row.

Howard Place – Robert Louis Stevenson

Robert Louis Stevenson was born at 8 Howard Place and lived there for three years before the family moved to 1 Inverleith Place (where they stayed for four years before moving again to 17 Heriot Row). A familiar scene for the young Stevenson was that recorded at Heriot Row some years later in his poem 'The Lamplighter':

Access

No. 8 Howard Place, off Inverleith Row – a private house.

My tea is nearly ready, and the sun has left the sky;
It's time to take the window to see Leerie [the
    lamplighter] going by;
For every night at tea-time and before you take your
    seat,
With lantern and with ladder he comes posting
    up the street.

Access

Inverleith Row/Howard Place.

Warriston Crescent, No. 10

Frédéric Chopin, the Polish composer, gave his only concert in Edinburgh at the Hopetoun Rooms (now Erskine House at 68–73 Queen Street) on Wednesday 4 October 1848. During his visit to Edinburgh Chopin stayed with Dr Adam Lyszcynski (a Polish medical graduate of the University of Edinburgh) at his home at 10 Warriston Crescent. At this time Chopin was still grieving over his recent separation from George Sand the novelist. The Edinburgh weather was generally cold and breezy and Chopin's visit was, all in all, a miserable one. He did, however, find time to compose one piece of music while he was there, a song called 'The Spring' (perhaps a gesture of hope?).

Access

No. 1 Queen Street.

Scottish National Portrait Gallery

The construction of the Scottish National Portrait Gallery (1890) was made possible by a gift of £50,000 from J.R. Findlay, proprietor of *The Scotsman*. His aim was to build up a visual record of Scots men and women of outstanding significance. The Scottish Photography Archive is also located in the gallery, while the gallery restaurant is well known for excellent food. At the Mound, the National Gallery, with its new Playfair extension, exhibits both Scottish and European art, while the Gallery of Modern Art and the Dean Gallery (both at Belford Road) are devoted to contemporary painting and sculpture. A free shuttle bus is available between the galleries.

Access

At 9 Queen Street; entry is free but needs to be arranged in advance with the librarian.

Royal College of Physicians

Charles II granted the college's first royal charter in 1681: the intention of the twenty-one original Fellows was not only to advance the practice of medicine but to improve prevention of disease and the care of patients (especially among the poor).

Originally housed in Fountain Close off the High Street, the college built a new hall in George Street (designed by James Craig) and moved there in 1781. However, the building was sold in 1834 and soon after demolished. Today the college has substantial premises at 9 Queen Street, a building completed in 1846.

On the great staircase are a bust by William Brodie of Sir James Young Simpson (1811–70, the discoverer of the anaesthetic properties of chloroform, who lived at 52 Queen Street); a portrait of Simpson (President of the College, 1850–2) by Norman Macbeth (1871), and a portrait of Alexander Wood (1817–84), also a President, by John Watson Gordon (1861). Dr Wood was the first man in Scotland to use a hypodermic needle for the relief of pain. On the first-floor landing is the college officer's staff topped by the cockerel of Aesculapius (the Greek god of medicine) and entangled by the sacred snake; on the wall are two large bronze Roman oil-lamps (also surmounted by the cockerel – this being the animal sacrificed to Aesculapius).

In the hall rows of Corinthian pillars support an airy ceiling surrounded by plaster heads and statues showing the great names in classical and Scottish medicine. Around the walls busts and paintings create a shining pantheon of medicine. At the south end of the hall are portraits of James VI and his queen, Anne of Denmark (probably by Cornelius Janssen); it was in James's reign that the first (unsuccessful) attempts were made to obtain incorporation for an independent Royal College of Physicians of Edinburgh. Under Charles II (whose portrait is also displayed) this was achieved.

Dr Archibald Pitcairne (1652–1713) has pride of place in the centre of the south wall. The youngest Fellow at the time of the foundation of the College, he was a man with a deep and original mind, and sometime Professor of Physic at Leyden in Holland (where Edinburgh doctors were trained before education in medicine was available in Scotland).

Another luminary was Dr James Gregory (1753–1821), who was President from 1798 to 1801. He was a member of an extraordinary family of academics, eight of whom were professors. James Gregory invented 'Gregory's Mixture' (made from rhubarb, ginger and magnesia), a medicine that remained popular for many years. Also on display is Raeburn's portrait of Andrew Duncan (President 1790 and 1824), one of the most influential Edinburgh physicians who had a hand in the foundation of many institutions, most notably the Royal Edinburgh Hospital for Psychiatric Disorders.

Sir Robert Philip (1857–1939) studied medicine at Edinburgh and later in Berlin with the discoverer of the tubercule bacillus, Professor Koch. He founded the Victoria Dispensary for Consumption in Bank Street, Edinburgh, in 1887. He was President of the Royal College of Physicians (1918–23) and Professor of Tuberculosis at Edinburgh University. His portrait in the College is by Sir James Guthrie.

The New Library contains the college's greatest treasure – Prince Charlie's medicine chest, a travelling chest which belonged to Sir Stuart Thriepland (1716–1805; President 1766–70). The heavy mahogany chest holds 160 remedies and many miniature instruments. It is probably French and is said to have been brought from France by the prince. Sir James Young Simpson's medicine box is also on view.

Among other treasures are a document recording the placing of the Scottish crown jewels in Edinburgh Castle; the first insurance policy for the college's books (signed by James Boswell's uncle, Dr John Boswell, President in 1770–2) and a letter of acknowledgement from Earl Haig when he was given an Honorary Fellowship.

In 8 Queen Street the first-floor reception rooms are probably the finest Adam rooms in Edinburgh. In the Fellows' Room are two portraits of Sir Robert Sibbald (1641–1722), founder of the college, and the pestle and mortar of William Cullen (1710–90), Professor of Chemistry at Edinburgh.

George Street – The Assembly Rooms

Access

George Street (south side).

The Assembly Rooms in George Street (not to be confused with the Church of Scotland's Assembly Hall on the Mound) were designed by John Henderson and first opened on Thursday 11 January 1787 with a ball held by the Caledonian Hunt. The new Assembly Rooms were the largest in Britain (except for those in Bath), being 92 feet long, 42 feet broad and 30 feet high. The 60-strong membership of the Caledonian Hunt consisted of 17 noblemen, 11 baronets and various others (mostly gentlemen with very large estates). Each member was allocated two ladies' tickets and one gentleman's: in all about 340 people attended. At the time of the opening of the Assembly Rooms the poet Robert Burns was in Edinburgh to oversee the printing of a new edition of his poems. The Caledonian Hunt had agreed to subscribe for a hundred copies and allowed Burns to dedicate his volume to the hunt. Burns himself, however, does not seem to have been invited. At the ball the ladies wore gowns of different coloured satins, covered with crêpe and ornamented with flowers. The most popular form of feminine headgear was the cap,

although turbans with feathers were to be seen as well as several pink Spanish hats.

As the supper room was not yet completed the tables were laid in the large room and the company danced in the tea room and also in the card rooms; it appears from the newspaper report that a certain amount of rowdy behaviour took place. There were certainly no minuets danced that night. At 4am the ladies went home but the gentlemen continued revelling until 8 o'clock.

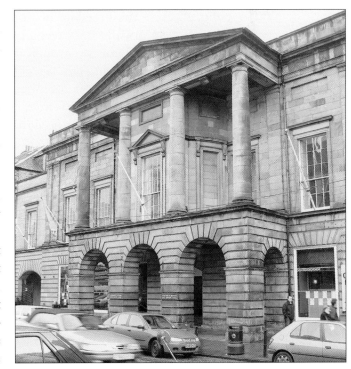

Along with the Hopetoun Rooms in Queen Street, the Assembly Rooms were the major venue for dinners and concerts. It was in the Assembly Rooms, for example, on 23 February 1827, at a benefit dinner for retired actors, that Sir Walter Scott dumbfounded the company with the news that he was 'the Great Unknown' – the anonymous author of the popular Waverley Novels. 'The effect was electrical,' reported *The Scotsman*, 'and, as soon as those present recovered from their surprise, they gave vent to their feelings in shouts of applause.'

In January 1841 the 29-year-old Hungarian pianist Franz Liszt gave a concert at the Assembly Rooms; he complained that the piano was a semitone sharp and then (to warm his frozen hands) performed what he called 'frightening the piano' with a very showy waltz which was not well received. On the following day he performed at the Hopetoun Rooms and then turned up at a concert given by the other artists in his party (four singers and instrumentalists), arriving late with 'some very dashing Scottish girls', completely unnerving his fellow-musicians by commenting adversely on their performances at the top of his voice. He was later observed enjoying himself in a Grassmarket tavern.

Charles Dickens first came to Edinburgh in 1834 as a journalist for the *Morning Chronicle*. In 1841 he was a member of the Scott Monument Committee and in that year was made a Freeman of the City at the Assembly Rooms, returning on several occasions to Edinburgh to give readings at the Music Hall.

George Street – The Music Hall

Access

Part of the Assembly Rooms complex, built on at the rear. Both are administered by the City of Edinburgh Council and frequently host public concerts, fairs or conferences. Those intending to visit should consult the caretaker in the first instance, whose office is located in the entrance hall.

In October 1843 the Music Hall (designed by David Bryce and William Burn) was built behind the Assembly Rooms. The new hall was in the shape of a cross with arms of equal length. To the south was the stage, to the north a U-shaped gallery.

The Music Hall was used for many public events, both artistic and political. Here the Freedom of Edinburgh was granted to Benjamin Disraeli (1867) while in November 1879 William Ewart Gladstone launched his Midlothian campaign there. In 1866 Thomas Carlyle was installed in the Music Hall as Rector of Edinburgh University (the McEwan Hall had not yet been built). In both world wars the Music Hall was used as a recruiting centre.

Cultural events are also a significant part of the Music Hall's programmes. Jenny Lind (1820–87), the 'Swedish Nightingale', sang in the Music Hall on six occasions (twice in 1847, three times in 1856 and in Haydn's *Creation* with the Choral Union in 1861). On her first appearance the crowd outside the Music Hall hooted at the audience as they passed into the concert-room and then threw stones at the windows, breaking some of them. Inside, the enthusiasm was so great that there were even people on the attic roof of the Music Hall staring down through the opening made for the great glass chandelier. During a moment's pause in one of Miss Lind's arias the clear but powerful voice of a Newhaven fishwife floated in from the street through the open windows with the cry 'Caller Ou' (fresh oysters); the great singer paused, listened attentively, and then told the audience 'That is a real voice.'

Queen Street – Sir James Young Simpson

Access

Simpson House belongs to the Church of Scotland and is part of its social service arm.

At the western end of Queen Street is no. 52, from 1845 until the year of his death the home of Sir James Young Simpson (1811–70). Chambers' *Biographical Dictionary* records that: 'In his house and at his table there were always to be found men and women of all countries, classes, opinions, and pursuits.' The discovery of the anaesthetic properties of chloroform was made here in 1847, as Simpson himself describes: 'I had the chloroform beside me for several days, but it seemed so unlikely a liquid to produce results of any kind, that it was laid aside; and on searching for another object among some loose papers, after coming home very late one night, my hand chanced to fall upon it; and I poured some of the fluid into tumblers before my assistants, Dr George Keith and Dr Duncan, and myself. Before sitting down to supper we all inhaled the fluid, and were all under the mahogany in a trice, to my wife's consternation and alarm.'

Overlooking the west end of Princes Street, at the edge of Princes Street Gardens, is a statue of Dr Simpson.

Queen Street – John Wilson and Francis Jeffrey

Access

A private dwelling.

Next door, at 53 Queen Street lived Professor John Wilson (1785–1854), before moving to Ann Street in 1819 and to Gloucester Place in 1825.

Here 'Christopher North' (Wilson's pen-name in *Blackwood's Magazine*) dreamed up the 'Chaldee Manuscript', a Biblical story supposed to be the translation of a recently unearthed manuscript, but in fact a thinly disguised satire on Edinburgh personalities, which was published in the October 1817 edition of *Blackwood's Magazine*. In 1820 Wilson managed (largely because of his Tory political connections) to have himself elected Professor of Moral Philosophy at Edinburgh University. This was a subject he knew next to nothing about, and he had to rely on regular letters sent from an old friend in England for his lecture-notes, often with comical results. Wilson's statue can be seen striking a dramatic pose at East Princes Street Gardens.

Francis, Lord Jeffrey (1773–1850) was living at 62 Queen Street at the time when the Whig *Edinburgh Review*, of which he was editor, was first printed (1802). His apartments were third-rate but Jeffrey, after a morning at the courts in Parliament House, spent his afternoons receiving clients and, as Archibald Constable noted, 'would write law pleadings, dine out, attend his evening parties, flutter with the lively and the gay, pay homage to beauty, till the night was far spent, and then return home to write an article for a *Review*, until the morning light found him still awake and working in his study'. Jeffrey rose through the legal profession, becoming Lord Advocate in 1830. He is buried beside Lord Cockburn in the Dean Cemetery.

WESTERN NEW TOWN

The Hopetoun Rooms

Designed by Thomas Hamilton (1827), the Hopetoun Rooms were once Edinburgh's finest concert hall. In January 1841 the Hungarian virtuoso pianist Franz Liszt gave a recital here and delighted his audience by playing on themes as they were suggested to him by members of the audience.

Seven years later in October 1848 the Polish composer and pianist Frédéric Chopin gave a two-hour evening concert at the Hopetoun Rooms. *The Scotsman* wrote that 'the infinite delicacy and finish of his playing, combined with great occasional energy never overdone, is very striking when we contemplate the man – a slender and delicate-looking person, with a marked profile, indicating much intellectual energy'.

The *Edinburgh Advertiser* added: 'while all other pianists strive to equalise the power of the fingers, M. Chopin aims to utilise them and, in accordance with this idea, are his treatment of the scale and the shake, as well as his mode of sliding with one and the same finger, from note to note, and of passing the third over the fourth finger'. Most of the elite of Edinburgh society were present and one critic noted that 'we have rarely seen such a display of rank and beauty congregated at a similar entertainment'.

Chopin did not neglect his fellow-countrymen in the audience: he played two Polish melodies 'somewhat peculiar in style, yet very pleasing. That they went home to the hearts of such of the performer's compatriots as were present, was evident from the delight with which they hailed each forgotten melody.'

In 1870 the Merchant Maiden Hospital (Mary Erskine's School) took over the building. In 1964 the classical façade of 1913 was replaced by a contemporary building to form the present Erskine House.

Access

On the southern side of Albyn Place (a western continuation of Queen Street).

Access

From the western end of
George Street. The
house is now occupied
by a private legal firm
but a small copy of the
statue under the Scott
Monument can be seen
above the door.

North Castle Street – Sir Walter Scott

Sir Walter Scott moved into his new home at 39 North Castle Street in 1798 and was to stay there for twenty-eight years. 'Scott's house in Edinburgh is divinely situated,' the poet Samuel Taylor Coleridge noted, 'it looks up a street full upon the rock and castle.'

In this house, sitting in his study behind the dining-room, Scott finished his novels *Waverley* (1814) and *Guy Mannering* (1815) and, in one year (1823), completed *Peveril of the Peak*, *Quentin Durward* and *St Ronan's Well*.

Every morning, Scott (a solicitor) worked as a Writer to the Signet at Parliament House and then spent the rest of the day writing. Scott, who was well over 6 feet tall, wrote seated in his study at a massive table, with the help of a fine old box richly carved and lined with red velvet. Only one picture brightened the gloomy room, depicting John Graham of Claverhouse (1648–89); it hung above the fireplace, with a Highland targe (shield) on either side, with broadswords and dirks radiating from them.

Access

At junction of North
Charlotte Street and St
Colme Street.

North Charlotte Street – Catherine Sinclair

Catherine Sinclair (1800–64) was the author of a number of popular children's books (*Holiday House*, for example), who also showed her concern for people less well off than herself by setting up a mission-station in Edinburgh and maintaining a large industrial school to prepare girls for domestic service. She gave pensions to the elderly, and formed a volunteer company of craftsmen with its own uniform, drill sergeant and band of musicians. She was the first to set

up a public fountain in the city and the first to introduce cooking depots (one in the Old Town and one in the New); she also took a special interest in the welfare of cab-drivers.

Charlotte Square – Sir Leander Starr Jameson

Access

Now the offices of the National Trust for Scotland.

No. 5 Charlotte Square (now occupied by the National Trust for Scotland) was the birth-place of Sir Leander Starr Jameson (1853–1917), whose father was a Writer to the Signet. Jameson studied medicine in Edinburgh and London before going to South Africa in 1878 as a partner in a medical practice in Kimberley, the gold-mining town, where he met the young Cecil Rhodes. Dr Jameson resigned his medical practice in 1889 to set off with a trader to deliver rifles and ammunition to Lobengula, King of the Matabele (whom he cured of gout).

In the famous Jameson Raid (1895) he made an unsuccessful attempt to come to the assistance of the Outlanders (who were in dispute with the Boer government) at the head of 600 men. Ambushed by the Boers at Krugersdorp, he and his remaining 250 men were surrounded by 3,000 Boers. After Jameson's surrender he was sentenced to be shot but President Kruger refused to sign the order. The Jameson Raid was, however, the spark that eventually led to the Boer War (1899–1902), after which Dr Jameson became Progressive Premier of the Cape Colony and was made a baronet in 1911.

The Georgian House

Access

On the north side of Charlotte Square, a fascinating paid-entry living museum of eighteenth-century Edinburgh life.

The Georgian House is part of the elegant yet simple façade created in 1790 by the architect Robert Adam at the suggestion of the Lord

Provost. Charlotte Square was the final section of the First New Town; the feus (plots of land) of the north side were put on sale in 1792, only a few days after Adam's death. The house at no. 7 was built in 1796 and sold to John Lamont. In 1975 it was opened to the public as a restored National Trust property. The Georgian House is designed to make visitors feel as if its eighteenth-century occupiers were still in residence: it has a 'lived-in' air to it. In the dining-room sideboard is that ultimate convenience: a pewter chamber pot (which was used quite unselfconsciously at table by the gentlemen after the ladies had left the room). The George III 'dumb waiters' (small two-tiered tables) were essential for guests when the servants were sent out of the room (so as not to overhear private conversations). Supplying the needs of the family was the commodious kitchen in the basement. This has been fitted out as it might once have been.

West Register House

In the centre of the west side of Charlotte Square is West Register House, designed as a church by Robert Reid. Dating from 1814, its dome is modelled on that of St Paul's Cathedral. Today it houses maps, plans, twentieth-century government records, railway records, those of the nationalised industries, legal records post-1800 and the private archives of industry and commerce. It also contains the Scottish Record Office Museum.

Among the documents often on display to the public are the Treaty of Edinburgh of 1328 negotiated by Robert I and Edward III of England; an inventory of the embroideries of Mary, Queen of Scots; the charges of witchcraft against Janet Boynan of the Cowgate who was convicted and burnt in 1572; a letter from Oliver Cromwell to Lieutenant-General David Leslie, commander of the Covenanter army, concerning the exchange of prisoners and the Articles of Union between England and Scotland (1706).

Among the personal letters on view are some from Robert Adam, James Boswell, Robert Burns, David Hume, Sir Henry Raeburn, Adam Smith, Robert Louis Stevenson, Thomas Telford and James Watt.

Charlotte Square – Henry, Lord Cockburn

On the west side of the square is no. 14 where Henry, Lord Cockburn (1779–1854), lived from 1812 to 1830. A key figure in the cultural history of Edinburgh, he was a writer of absorbing memoirs with a genius for the description of character. 'Cockburn', wrote Dr Thomas Guthrie, 'was a man of fascinating manners and fine genius; the greatest orator, in one sense, I ever heard.' Thomas Carlyle gives this picture: 'a bright, cheery-voiced, large-eyed man, a Scotch dialect with plenty of good logic in it'. The *Edinburgh Review* in 1857 added that he was 'rather below the middle height, firm, wiry and muscular, inured to active exercise of all kinds, a good swimmer, an accomplished skater, and an intense lover of the fresh breezes of heaven'. Cockburn was Solicitor-General in 1830 and seven years later a Lord of Justiciary. As one of the leaders of the Scottish Whigs he helped draft the First Reform Bill for Scotland. The rest of his days he spent in his country seat at Bonaly and, at his death, was buried in the Dean Cemetery.

Charlotte Square – Earl Haig

Access

Now a private residence.

At the west corner of the southern side of Charlotte Square (at no. 24) Field-Marshal Lord Douglas Haig (1861–1928) was born. After schooling at Clifton and Brasenose College, Oxford, Haig went to Sandhurst in 1883 before being sent to India with the 7th Hussars. He failed the examinations for the Staff College and suffered from colour blindness, but his career was meteoric. He served in the Omdurman campaign in 1898 and in the Boer War. He was appointed major-general in 1904 and then went to the War Office in 1906 as Director of Military Training.

At the time of the First World War he took two divisions to France and enhanced his reputation as a leader at the First Battle of Ypres. He was subsequently made Commander-in-Chief. Although he had courage and showed skill in directing the battles in France, he arguably failed to be aware of the tactical situation on the ground and risked the lives of many of his men where there was little real chance of success. After the war he worked tirelessly for the development of the Royal British Legion and the United Services Fund. His equestrian statue stands on Edinburgh Castle Esplanade.

Charlotte Square – Alexander Graham Bell

Access

Now a private residence.

It was at 16 South Charlotte Street that Alexander Graham Bell (1847–1922), inventor of the tele-phone, first saw the light of day. He was a pupil at the High School (1858–62) and then moved to London. Alexander's father was a professor of elocution, who chal-lenged his son to make a speaking machine. This he and his brother did, building it out of a lamb's larynx, using rubber sheeting and a gutta-percha moulding of the human skull and jawbone. To this were added rubber lips, a wooden tongue and a soft palate stuffed with cottonwool. By blowing into a metal tube, the brothers were able to make the head say 'Mama' so convincingly that the neighbours were heard to ask: 'What can be the matter with the baby?'

Charlotte Square – Sir Robert Philip

Access

Now a private residence.

From 1898 until 1938 no. 45 Charlotte Square (on the north-east side of the square) was the home of Sir Robert Philip (1857–1939), who was largely responsible for the conquest of the killer disease tuberculosis. Philip studied medicine at Edinburgh and after further research in 1887 opened the Victoria Dispensary for Consumption in Bank Street (off the Lawnmarket), developing what became known as the 'Edinburgh System' of visiting homes where cases of tuberculosis had been found. By 1894 the clinic had become the Royal Victoria Hospital for Consumption.

Sir Robert Philip was knighted in 1913 and became President of the Royal College of Physicians and Professor of Tuberculosis at Edinburgh University four years later.

The Dean Village

Access

Off Queensferry Street and the Dean Bridge, down Bell's Brae.

Formerly a flour-milling community and tannery deep in a valley known as the Water of Leith Village, the Dean Village became a forgotten backwater after the construction of the nearby Dean Bridge (1830). Other misfortunes befell the village: the tannery closed around 1970 and a disastrous fire in May 1957 famously destroyed around 100,000 stored theatrical costumes and thousands of stage backcloths and props and other riches of William Mutrie & Son, the theatrical costumier, once the largest firm of its kind outside London. On a larger scale the Dean Village remains, like Swanston Village, suspended in time, with its curious architectural flourishes and stunning views over the Water of Leith. It also boasts one of the last Queen Victoria letterboxes marked 'V.R.'

NORTHERN NEW TOWN

Drummond Place – James M. Barrie

The writer J.M. Barrie (1860–1937) was born in Kirriemuir, Angus, the son of a weaver. From 1879 to 1882 during his student days at Edinburgh University he lodged in the top flat of the north-facing West House at 3 Great King Street. The author of *Peter Pan* (1904), *The Admirable Crichton* (1902) and *Dear Brutus* (1917) as a struggling student saw a seamier side of life. In his *Better Dead* Barrie gives a harrowing but impartial account of conditions in his student 'digs': 'I knew three undergraduates who lodged together in a dreary house at the top of a dreary street; two of them used to study until two in the morning, while the third slept. When they shut up their books they wake number three, who arose, dressed and studied until breakfast time. Among the many advantages of this arrangement the chief was that, as they were dreadfully poor, one bed did for three – if lodgings were cheap and dirty, and dinners few and far between, life was still real and earnest; in many cases it did not turn out an empty dream.' Elsewhere Barrie describes his student rooms in greater detail: 'To turn up the light on old college days is not always the signal for the dance. You are back in the dusty little lodging, with its tattered sofa, its slippery tablecloth, the prim array of books, the picture of the death of Nelson, the peeling walls, the broken clock; you are again in the quadrangle with him who has been dead this many a year.'

Access

Now a private dwelling-house at the west corner of Drummond Place, off Dublin Street, at the east end of Queen Street.

Author of *Confessions of an English Opium-eater* (1822) Thomas De Quincey (1785–1859), lodged at 9 Great King Street (1830–4). A prolific contributor to *Blackwood's Magazine*, the *Edinburgh Literary Gazette* and *Tait's Edinburgh Magazine*, he lived in Edinburgh and district between 1820 and his death: on 27 November 1833 and 24 November 1836, however, he was lodged in the Debtors Sanctuary at Holyroodhouse, allowed to go safely into Edinburgh to visit his friends only on Sundays.

Heriot Row – Robert Louis Stevenson

Access

On the north side of Queen Street Gardens.

From the age of six Robert Louis Stevenson (1850–94) lived at 17 Heriot Row with its views over Queen Street Gardens up to the august heights of the New Town. He was often taken to play in the gardens by his devoted nurse 'Cummy' (Alison Cunningham), and he liked to meander along the Water of Leith or wander through the mysterious groves of Warriston Cemetery. As he was confined to bed by illness for

long periods, Stevenson's imagination would be fired by folk tales or adventure stories told on the 'land of counterpane', the wonderful make-believe world in the hillocks and valleys of his childhood eiderdown. It was his early life at 17 Heriot Row that provided the inspiration for *A Child's Garden of Verses*. In his *Nuits Blanches* Stevenson wrote: 'I remember, so long ago, the sickly child that woke from his few hours' slumber with the sweat of a nightmare on his brow, to lie awake and listen and long for the first signs of life among the silent streets. Over the black belt of the garden I saw the long line of Queen Street, with here and there a lighted window. The road before our house is a great throughfare for early carts. You can hear the carters cracking their whips and crying hoarsely to their horses.'

Access

Between Heriot Row and Royal Circus.

India Street – James Clerk Maxwell

The scientist James Clerk Maxwell (1831–79) was born at 14 India Street, the son of a lawyer who also had a keen interest in geology. In far-off Galloway (where James spent his earliest years), his father encouraged him to make collections of insects, rocks and flowers.

As a student at Edinburgh Academy, Maxwell (who had a stutter and was small for his age) was nicknamed Dafty by the other boys because of his Galloway accent. Despite this, he successfully laid the foundations for a more mature curiosity: when he was just fifteen his first research paper was read to the Royal Society of Edinburgh and in the following year he became a student at Edinburgh University.

After Edinburgh he went to Cambridge where he produced two major scientific breakthroughs: he established the foundation of the modern measurement of colour and showed the way to a theory of electro-magnetism which predicted the existence of waves travelling at the speed of light and made up of magnetic and electrical fields. James Clerk Maxwell therefore provided the theoretical and practical tools for the development of radio, radar and television.

Gloucester Lane – David Roberts

Access

Today commercial premises at the junction of Gloucester Lane and Doune Terrace.

Duncans Land in Gloucester Lane is now a restaurant but in 1796 it was the birthplace of the artist David Roberts (1796–1864). His father was a shoemaker but young David showed early artistic talent (developed with charcoal on the whitewashed kitchen wall of their home) and so, at the age of twelve, he was apprenticed to a painter and decorator.

During the years of his apprenticeship Roberts learnt all the tricks of the trade: how to give the illusion of marble, wood or even that of a three-dimensional scene. When he qualified as a journeyman, Roberts was hired by a travelling circus to restore their scenic backcloths and paint new ones. This was invaluable training in a more flamboyant pictorial style and good preparation for his next employment – as a scene-painter for a number of British theatres (he had even, in emergencies, appeared on stage).

Returning to Edinburgh in 1818 he was commissioned by Francis Jeffrey to re-decorate his library at Craigcrook Castle; he was also employed at the Theatre Royal at the east end of Princes Street.

After being engaged by Covent Garden Opera House as a designer, he was elected President of the Society of British Artists. In the years that followed Roberts travelled to the continent and to Egypt, returning with magnificent paintings of landscapes and scenery which were duly engraved and proved to be enormously popular.

Ann Street – Ann Raeburn

Access

Either from Queensferry Road or from Stockbridge.

Ann Street is believed to be named after Sir Henry Raeburn's wife, Ann Edgar, a rich widow. The first purchase of land for building took place in 1814, and Ann Street, with its rural charm, is said to be the most beautiful street in Edinburgh.

Access

Inverleith Row (to the
east) or Arboretum
Place (to the west)

The Royal Botanic Garden

The story of the Royal Botanic Garden is one of successful growth and fruitful migration. Near Holyroodhouse in 1670 Robert Sibbald and Andrew Balfour, two Edinburgh doctors, filled a 12-yard square plot with medicinal herbs and plants; it was only the second botanic garden in Britain. In 1684 the doctors opened a second Physic Garden at Trinity Hospital (now occupied by Waverley station booking-office). The two gardens were united on a new site in 1763 (near the top of Leith Walk) and then in 1820 transferred north to the present (larger) location at Inverleith, in an operation lasting three years.

The purpose of the Physic Garden was to grow herbs and flowers to make medicines. In the modern Royal Botanic Garden the old Holyrood Garden Bell can still be seen today at the Herbarium reception at 20A Inverleith Row; until 1970 the bell was rung in the Botanic Garden at the start and end of every working day. It is believed that it was commissioned in London by James VI in 1607 for Holyroodhouse and was later used in the original Physic Garden. Dr John Hope became Regius Keeper of the two gardens, united the Royal and Town Gardens and transferred the whole collection of plants to one location (at the top of Leith Walk). There he classified the plants according to the new system of the Swedish botanist Carl Linnaeus (1707–78), and erected a monument (designed by Robert Adam in 1778) to Linnaeus which still stands today in the present Botanic Garden.

The focal point of the new site is Inverleith House (1774), now used as an exhibition area; the Tropical Palm House (1834) and the Temperate Palm House (1858) are notable for the curved patterns of their glazed roofs while the New Glass Houses (1967) achieve a maximum of glass by the use of braced tension-cables.

(By permission of the Royal Botanic Garden)

Inverleith House

At the heart of the Royal Botanic Garden's inventively designed landscape stands Inverleith House. In the sixteenth century the Touris family were the Lords of Inverleith. Their estate lay north and west of Edinburgh, circling round the south side of the Castle Rock.

A century later the estate of Inverleith became the property of the Rocheids who took up residence there. One of the family, Sir James Rocheid, was Town Clerk of Edinburgh in 1668. As a public official he had a career that verged on the criminal. He was suspected of embezzling from the proceeds of Edinburgh's duty on ale and beer and he was believed to have interfered with the annual Town Council elections. Sir James was eventually dismissed from his post, but later reinstated.

In Sir James's time the long entrance to the house wound down the hill to the Water of Leith and ran alongside the river to St Bernard's Row at Stockbridge. The first house had fallen into ruins by the time one of his descendants, James Rocheid, had the present house built in 1774. With three storeys, and a basement by David Henderson, the interior was partly refinished (after a fire) by W.W. Robertson in 1877. In 1960 further changes were made to its structure when it became the National Gallery of Modern Art. In 1984 the gallery moved to the former John Watson's School in Belford Road and Inverleith House was devoted primarily to exhibitions related to the work of the Royal Botanic Garden.

The details of the construction of the house are of considerable interest as they show the contribution made by an army of workmen.

(By permission of the Royal Botanic Garden)

The house, designed by the architect David Henderson, was built with stone from the Craigleith quarry and with locally made brick. Some 66 stones of lead was used to cover the roof. The detailed estimates and accounts which have survived show that the wright (carpenter) responsible for much of the woodwork was James Watson of Canonmills. Glazier Thomas Reikie fitted not only common glass but also the best Newcastle Crown glass in the main windows. The brickmakers were led by Isaac Mullender, while Samuel Richardson was in charge of laying the bricks; George Syme was the master-slater and William Kinghorn oversaw the transportation of countless cart-loads of materials such as rubble stone, pend stone and flagstone. James Paterson was the sawyer, William Scot laid the causey (road); the craftsman who worked the marble inside the building was Alexander White, while the plasterer-in-chief was Robert Whitehead.

Some 800 pounds of iron ballusters were purchased to make the rail which ran up the inside stair and 433 feet of 2-inch wood was needed to build the sash windows. The interior was decorated with Dutch white tiles. One of the joiners spent one day and seven hours hanging doors, for which he received 2 shillings and 4 pence. The tile-setter was paid 2 shillings and 6 pence a day and the plasterer 1 shilling and 8 pence. The workman who put down the road leading to the house received 1 shilling a day and his assistant 10 pence.

Perhaps the most arresting person who ever lived in the house was James Rocheid's mother, who drove out in her mulberry-coloured coach to the dancing assemblies at Buccleuch Place over which she majestically presided. Lord Cockburn has left a memorable description of Mrs Rocheid which makes her almost as fascinating as the most attractive of modern flowers in the Botanic Garden today: 'Nobody could sit down like the lady of Inverleith. She would sail like a ship from Tarshish, gorgeous in velvet or rustling in silk and managing all this seemingly heavy rigging with as much ease as a full-blown swan does its plumage, she would take possession of a large sofa and, without the slightest visible exertion, would cover the whole of it with her bravery, the graceful folds seeming to lay themselves over it like summer waves.'

From 1863 to 1874 the occupant of the house was the legal historian Cosmo Innes, whose daughter recorded her father's bountiful hospitality: 'Visitors never seemed to cease. From morn to night the beautiful croquet lawn was bright with smart young figures and the nacking sound of croquet-balls. In the evenings the handsome reception rooms were often crowded with parties assembled for music and dancing.'

Two years after Cosmo Innes's death in 1874 Edinburgh Town Council bought the house with its gardens and parkland to form an arboretum, which was transferred to the Crown (along with the house) as an addition to the Royal Botanic Garden. The house then became the official residence of the Regius Keeper of the Garden, who was also Professor of Botany at Edinburgh University.

OUTER EDINBURGH

OUTER EDINBURGH (SOUTH)

Royal Lyceum Theatre

Access

No. 30B Grindlay Street.

The Royal Lyceum Theatre opened on 10 September 1883, and Henry Irving and Ellen Terry starred in the first production, Shakespeare's *Much Ado about Nothing*. The ceremonial opening began with some spontaneous choral singing and then the iron safety curtain went up. During the play Irving and Terry charmed the audience.

Irving had first come to Edinburgh in 1857 when only 19 years of age and spent two years at the Theatre Royal in Shakespeare Square (now the east end of Princes Street). While at the Lyceum he stayed in the Edinburgh Hotel opposite the Waverley Bridge and was often to be seen in a rough loose-fitting pepper-and-salt tweed suit, studying his roles as he walked up Arthur's Seat or over the Calton Hill. A century later the character actor Wilfrid Lawson, playing in Sean O'Casey's *Cock-a-Doodle Dandy* at the Lyceum (1959), recalled that: 'It must have been over thirty years ago that I combined the learning of golf and the playing of Shaw in a six-week season at Edinburgh.' In the same year Dame Edith Sitwell gave readings there and complained: 'I travelled up here by train and car and when I got here I was on the verge of whining with fatigue.'

Usher Hall

Access

Lothian Road.

The circular, copper-domed Usher Hall (1914) was built with a donation of £100,000 from the brewer Andrew Usher. Capable of holding an audience of 2,900, the Usher Hall has seen many of the greatest names in the world of music perform, from Sir Thomas Beecham to Mario Lanza.

Conducting in the Usher Hall in 1956, Sir Thomas produced at least two *bons mots* on the venue and Edinburgh concert-goers. Turning to an Usher Hall audience who clapped too soon, Sir Thomas exclaimed: 'I deeply regret we have not finished yet!' On the same occasion he added: 'Edinburgh Festival audiences applaud everything with equal in-discrimination!'

King's Theatre

Access

No. 2 Leven Street.

The art nouveau stained-glass panels on the doors of the King's Theatre (constructed 1905–6) entice you in with the promise of wonders to come once the lights are dimmed: variety, drama and opera have filled the auditorium. One enamelled door-handle is decorated with a blazing sun, the other with a bat (straight out of *Die Fledermaus* or *Dracula*).

Famously, during one Edinburgh Festival, Maria Callas appeared there and then suddenly left the country the following day. In 1966 Wendy Hiller, appearing in *A Present for the Past*, recalled: 'I was touring with the Bristol Old Vic during a harsh winter, when one night at the King's, during a full house, the trams went off because of the weather. We plodded home in Wellington boots and I think we were stranded here for about three days.'

McEwan Hall

Access

Bristo Square.

The McEwan Hall (1897), financed by Sir William McEwan, MP for the Central Division of Edinburgh (and chairman of the well-known Edinburgh firm of brewers), is part of Edinburgh University and is regularly used for graduations, graduands being capped with 'Geordie Buchanan's breeks' (the trousers of the eminent scholar and Reformation divine George Buchanan, sometime tutor to the young James VI and I). In 1909 the great Italian tenor Enrico Caruso sang in the McEwan Hall – five years before the Usher Hall was opened. Caruso was staying at the Caledonian Hotel, having arrived by rail. The singer appeared immensely pleased at being escorted from the then Caledonian station by a pipe band, provided by his impresario, and those who witnessed the scene long remembered the beaming face of the tall, broad-shouldered tenor as he strode through the station to the accompaniment of the roll of the drums and the skirl of pipes. So delighted was he with his reception that he at first proposed to appear at his concert dressed in full Highland costume and had to be dissuaded by his manager from taking such a potentially embarrassing decision.

Merchiston – Merchiston Castle

Access

At the centre of Napier University's complex on Colinton Road.

Merchiston Castle was the home of the Napier family and it was here that the polymath John Napier (1550–1617) was born. Napier's father was master of the Scottish Mint but his son showed mathematical talents of a different nature, later developed at the universities of St Andrews and Paris and broadened by travels in Germany and Italy.

Napier was deeply interested in theology as the central science of man's place in creation. In 1588 he was a Commissioner to the General Assembly of the Church of Scotland, while in 1593 he attacked the Church of Rome in his *Plaine Discovery of the Whole Revelation of St John*.

His researches into practical engineering were turned to military use: he designed a tank and a primitive 'laser' weapon using the sun's rays focused on to a mirror. He put forward new methods of land-use and experimented with chemical fertilisers.

He acquired a reputation for being something of a wizard because of his inventiveness and ingenuity but his greatest innovation was the development of logarithms (a method of calculating using rods or bones), as a way of increasing the speed and ease of making mathematical calculations. He can therefore be regarded as one of the forerunners of computer science. Today Merchiston Castle (which once housed Merchiston Castle School) forms the centrepiece of

(By permission of Napier University)

Napier University's first campus near Morningside, and is enhanced by a fine wooden painted ceiling of 1581 brought from Prestongrange, East Lothian, in 1964.

Canaan Lane – Sir Reginald Fleming Johnston

The Last Emperor, a film directed by Bernardo Bertolucci, is based on the life of Sir Reginald Fleming Johnston (1874–1938), who was born at Goshen Bank (a substantial and handsome villa at 24 Canaan Lane), the son of a solicitor.

Johnston was educated at Edinburgh University and at Oxford and entered the Hong Kong Civil Service in 1898. He became secretary to the government of Weihaiwei (1904–6), later acting as tutor to the last Xanchu Emperor, the young Pu Yi (1919–25). Johnston saved his pupil from life imprisonment (and probably death) in 1924 when he hid him in the British Legation from the 'Christian General' Feng Yu Hsiang.

Sir Reginald was the last Commissioner before the territory was returned to China in 1930. In the following year he became Professor of Chinese at London University. At his death in Edinburgh the Emperor of Manchuria (his former pupil) sent a message of sympathy.

Access

Goshen Bank is a private home and although the owners are happy to welcome visitors, every consideration should be shown by the latter.

Access

From Oxgangs Road
head south on
Swanston Road over the
motorway. Swanston
Cottage is a private
residence.

Swanston Cottage

Taking the new Swanston Road over the motorway towards the 'Anchor or T-Wood', the visitor turns right just before a cluster of farm steadings (small businesses with stables at the rear) and walks along the track to the south of the garden wall of the privately-owned Swanston Cottage, a small whitewashed two-storey building facing the Pentland Hills. The curious visitor should exercise sensitivity and caution, and avoid doing anything that would intrude into the privacy of the steadings or the cottage.

A black bell high on the west corner of the house sits under its own small wooden roof surmounted by a kingfisher with a long beak. A retaining wall in the garden is ornamented with fragments of Gothic stone tracery. From his bedroom on the first floor between 1867 and 1880 the author Robert Louis Stevenson must often have looked out at the scarred slopes of Caerketton Hill with its browsing sheep and spiky gorse bushes. He first came here as an engineering student, spending many hours on the hillside with book and notepad. Sometimes he would climb over to Rullion Green where the Covenanters had been savagely defeated by General Tam Dalyell and his government forces in 1666. Stevenson also crossed the hills to Glencorse to meditate at the graves of the Covenanters and many years later wrote of:

> Grey recumbent tombs of the dead in desert places
> Standing-stones on the vacant wine-red moor
> Hills of sheep, and the howes of the silent vanished races,
> And winds, austere and pure.

Pentland Hills: Swanston Village

Turning back to the main road, head up past the golf club into the car park and take the little path winding up through the trees. Suddenly it is as if you had stepped back into *Brigadoon*. Eighteenth-century cottages with white stone walls nestle among the nooks and crannies on each side of the path which leads upwards towards the hill beyond. Swanston Village is like a picturesque part of the Highlands concealed in the city!

There is a public path through the private cottages up to the hill.

Drummond Scrolls

Access

Remains of William Adam's original Drummond Street Royal Infirmary façade are to be found near Colinton in the quaintly named 'Drummond Scrolls' (on the east side of the road), with their extravagantly carved foliage and the eccentric Covenanters' Monument (on the other side of Redford Road) made from half-columns stuck together and saved from destruction by a local bailie.

A brief diversion away from central Edinburgh to a private residence halfway down Redford Road (off the city bypass). The owners are happy to show the exterior of their extraordinary home to members of the public who have a genuine interest.

Gilmerton Cove

In Gilmerton, below the floor of a betting office, an eighteenth-century drinking den is hidden in a grotto hewn out of the solid rock, part of a network of caves and tunnels. Graffiti covers the tables and there is even a carved punchbowl marked with Masonic symbols. Perhaps this was one of the favourite meeting-places of the notorious Hell-Fire Club, an association for wealthy young men high on testosterone, who conducted their private rituals by candlelight. The members of this legendary drinking-club gathered to womanise and sing bawdy songs. In those days the house above was a blacksmith's shop and documents have recently come to light which show that the blacksmith was summoned in front of the Kirk Session for selling alcohol on a Sunday. Today Gilmerton Cove is a popular tourist attraction.

Craigmillar – Craigmillar Castle

The earliest parts of Craigmillar Castle, a fortified stone tower, were built by the Preston family, who had taken possession of the barony in 1374. In its long history Craigmillar Castle was both a refuge and a prison: within its walls the Earl of Mar was secretly assassinated by his brother James III in 1477, while a young King James V was taken to Craigmillar in 1512 for about a month to escape an epidemic of throat infection at Edinburgh Castle.

During the English invasion of 1544 under the Earl of Hertford the castle was partly destroyed by the English cavalry. However, because of its situation close to the countryside and the sea, Craigmillar Castle was always a popular centre for hunting and so it was rebuilt. Mary, Queen of Scots and her husband Henry, Lord Darnley often stayed there to enjoy the hunting.

(By permission of Historic Scotland)

South of the castle is the area where Mary, Queen of Scots' French retainers lived, nicknamed 'Little France'. Until a few years ago an ancient tree stood by the roadside which was said to have been planted by Queen Mary herself, and French sorrel (a culinary herb) still grew beside the castle walls until fairly recently.

In 1566 Mary, Queen of Scots, sad and bewildered by the murder of her Italian secretary David Rizzio, hid herself away at Craigmillar. At the so-called Craigmillar Conference the Lords persuaded Mary to agree to 'dispose of' her husband Lord Darnley, insisting that it would be for the common good of the nation.

Mary's son King James VI was the last monarch to live at Craigmillar Castle, and there he planned his visit to Norway to bring back his young wife Anne of Denmark. Today Craigmillar Castle hosts festivities and a pageant as part of the annual Craigmillar Festival.

OUTER EDINBURGH (NORTH)

Leith

Access

From the foot of Leith Walk turn down Great Junction Street, travelling north.

Leith has an 800-year history as a commercial port, trading with Europe and the rest of the world. The Leith character is breezy and salty, full of generosity. To be a Leither is to be fiercely proud of an identity quite separate from Edinburgh's – but ignominiously surrendered in 1820 when the Burgh Port was amalgamated with its larger rival to the south (Edinburgh).

It was David I who, in 1128, first granted land and harbour rights to the Abbey of Holyroodhouse, rights which were confirmed by a charter of Robert I in 1329. South Leith was held by the Logans of Restalrig under Holyrood, while North Leith came under the direct administration of Holyrood Abbey. No foreign goods shipped into Leith could be sold there: they had to be taken up to the Edinburgh markets. By 1567 Edinburgh had become the feudal superior of South Leith (the larger half of the Burgh Port) and, around seventy years later, of North Leith. From 1567 to 1833 the bailies who sat in Leith Burgh Court to pass judgment on offenders were appointed by Edinburgh and did not as a rule even live in Leith (in the late eighteenth century the journey from Edinburgh to Leith

took an hour). Today, with the relative decline of commercial shipping, Leith has blossomed as a highly desirable and upmarket place to live and to be entertained, and there are many tourist attractions, notably the royal yacht *Britannia* at Ocean Terminal.

The Vaults

Leith Vaults provide two extraordinary culinary experiences in one historic location. On the ground floor is the Vintners' Room, the oldest premises in Scotland to remain in continuous commercial use. Constructed in the eleventh century, the cellars were used to store wine imported by the Augustinian monks at Holyrood. The Vintners' Room itself, previously the sale room of the Vintners' Guild, with its seventeenth-century plasterwork and auctioneers' alcove, today houses a distinguished restaurant. On the first floor the Scotch Malt Whisky Society's members' room provides a relaxed ambience for whisky tasting and entertainment.

Leith Council Chamber

At 75–81 Constitution Street and 29–41 Queen Charlotte Street Leith Town Hall and police station have proved to be popular attractions. Built as Leith Sheriff Court in 1828 (with reconstructions in 1868), the splendidly decorated and panelled chamber (with its portraits of civic dignitaries) has as its outstanding feature *Oh Happy Day*, a 12 × 6 foot panoramic painting by Alexander Carse (*c.* 1770–1843), which shows King George IV landing at Leith on 15 August 1822. (This visit restored the ebbing status of Scotland since 1603 and is therefore usually regarded as a landmark event.) In the painting sailors crowd the yard-arms of the berthed royal vessel, while the Royal Company of Archers stand in two lines holding their bows in salute and the Royal Dragoon Guards flourish their sabres. In the foreground, quite unnoticed, a young pickpocket is at work!

Access

Queen Charlotte Street, off Constitution Street. As this is part of a working police station visits by members of the public are strictly by arrangement only. For more information, contact the Leith Station Police Inspector on 0131 554 9350.

Access

A property at the foot of Leith Walk (99 Kirkgate), managed by Historic Scotland.

Trinity House

The story of Trinity House begins in about 1380 when a levy began to be made on every ton of merchandise loaded or unloaded by Scottish ships at the Port of Leith. The income from this levy was distributed to the poor. In 1483 Our Lady's Kirk of Leith was built not far off by the mariners and skippers of Leith and by 1566 a hospital or almshouse was erected on the site of the present building (this function was ratified by Mary, Queen of Scots and her husband Henry, Lord Darnley).

Some seventy years later it was necessary to set up an inquiry into the use of the funds and to formulate regulations. Letters from Charles II dated October 1636 and from James Prymrose, Clerk to the Privy Council (and father-in-law of George Heriot), are displayed to this day. The hospital became an incorporation in 1797 and in the same year the Freedom of the Incorporation was given to the newly victorious Admiral

Adam Duncan after the Battle of Camperdown against the Dutch. Admiral Duncan accepted the honour with gratitude and his portrait by Sir Henry Raeburn was commissioned by Trinity House (where it still hangs). Trinity House also displays the ancient strong-box Charter Chest together with the ballot-box of the incorporation.

On the first floor is the convening room, dominated by a gigantic painting of the explorer Vasco da Gama (1469–1525) doubling the Cape of Good Hope on his way to India (1497–8). There is also a print of Mary, Queen of Scots landing at Leith from France in 1561, and no fewer than four portraits by Sir Henry Raeburn, including one of Peter Wood, a whaleship owner and Bailie of Leith (aged 77 in 1826). Another print depicts the Suez Canal, through which a Leith-built ship, the SS *Danube*, commanded by Captain Charles Mann, made the first passage in November 1869, some time before the canal's official completion. On a large central table are two horns of a narwhal (sea-unicorn), believed to be an aphrodisiac, sailmakers' tools and part of the cable which connected Scotland and Norway (and which was repaired during the 1940 German occupation). Also to be seen is a photograph of the Tsar and Tsarina of Russia arriving at Leith on 22 September 1896.

Above the gate to the courtyard of Trinity House is a stone dated 1570 which bears a verse from Psalm 107:

> They that goe down to the sea in shippes
> That doe business in the great Waters
> These see the works of the Lord
> And his wanders in the deep.

Lauriston Castle

Access

North of Queensferry Road via Cramond Road South (turn right after Lauriston Farm Road).

John Law (1671–1729) was a pioneer of modern banking and founded a financial institution in France which paved the way for a French national bank. The son of a goldsmith, Law showed an early talent for figures – and gambling. In London he was caught up in a dispute over a woman and killed a man in a duel, an offence for which, in 1694, he was imprisoned and condemned to death. However, Law escaped and fled to Holland where he began to study Dutch banking practice. He then eloped with a married woman to Switzerland, where they married and then settled in Genoa. There he began speculating in foreign exchange and securities.

In 1703 Law returned to Edinburgh and set up home at Lauriston Castle, where he developed a plan to issue bank notes. This was rejected by the Scottish Parliament, so Law went to Paris where he developed a scheme for paying off the French national debt. In 1716 his proposal for a joint-stock bank was accepted by the French government. Law then set up a company to develop French commercial interests in North

(By permission of City of Edinburgh Council)

America. He ordered the construction of the future city of New Orleans and became the first 'millionaire'. In 1720 he was appointed controller-general of finance for the Kingdom of France. In the same year, however, an edict was issued which resulted in the devaluation of the French currency and led to the collapse of Law's 'system'. He was exiled and died in Venice in 1729.

Among the many other owners of the castle were Thomas Allan (1823), proprietor of the *Caledonian Mercury*, an Edinburgh newspaper, and Andrew Rutherford, Lord Advocate and MP for Leith Burghs. In 1902 the house was bought by businessman William Reid, a time-served cabinet-maker who had studied in London and Paris. Reid's firm specialised in furniture-making, in fitting out luxury railway carriages and ships and in architectural restoration. Reid's wife, moreover, was the daughter of the founder of a firm of sanitary engineers. Together they could call on all the craftsmen necessary to restore the castle and furnish it with the most up-to-date domestic appliances.

Thus Lauriston Castle has the latest central heating system of the time and the carpets used are identical to those in the best railway carriages. The zinc bath in the Reids' bathroom was the standard fitting for ocean liners, while the secondary glazing in the master bedroom was the latest fashion, as pioneered in Bavaria. Reid was also a connoisseur and a man of taste, and the castle contains his fine collection of Blue John, a translucent crystallised limestone (actually more brown and purple than blue). Throughout the house (which was greatly extended in the nineteenth century) genuine antique furniture stands side by side with modern reproductions designed and executed to the highest standards by Reid and his craftsmen.

Cramond Village

Access

From Queensferry Road via Cramond Road South.

Cramond is an oasis of charm, with the remains of a Roman fort, a seventeenth-century parish church, quaint houses and a local inn – and the chance, in summer, to be ferried in a rowing-boat across the mouth of the River Almond.

In 1997 ferryman Robert Graham unearthed a white sandstone lioness from the mud of the river. This was described as one of the most important Roman finds for decades in what is the earliest known Roman settlement, one of only three Scottish sites visited by the African-born Roman Emperor Septimus Severus, who used Cramond as the base for his campaign against the rebellious tribes in what is now Scotland.

(Copyright: F.C. Inglis)

Hawes Inn

Access

From Edinburgh, via Barnton, the A90 and the B924.

Hawes Inn lies on the shore of the River Forth at an ancient crossing-point north to Fife. Today the inn sits in the shadow of the historic Forth Rail Bridge. A sixteenth-century tavern, its abiding interest today is its appearance in the works of Robert Louis Stevenson, who often visited the inn as a student or after a hard day's canoeing on the Forth with Walter Simpson (son of Sir James Young Simpson, the discoverer of the anaesthetic properties of chloroform). Stevenson was also in the habit of walking along the shore of the River Forth at Granton, Cramond and South Queensferry, and it was on one of these walks that he first revealed to his father his desire to be a writer and not a lighthouse engineer. Although Sir Walter Scott had already mentioned Hawes Inn in his book *The Antiquary*, Stevenson in *Kidnapped* has David Balfour's Uncle Ebeneezer and Captain Hoseason of the brig *Covenant* plan Balfour's kidnap 'in a small room, with a bed in it and heated like an oven by a great fire of coal'. The book ends with David Balfour going to South Queensferry to find the lawyer Mr Rankeillor in order to unravel his and Alan Breck's problems.

Outer Edinburgh (East)

St Triduana's Well

Access

Restalrig Road South
(below Jock's Lodge and
Meadowbank Stadium).
Keys may be obtained
from the church building
between 11.00am and
1.00pm Monday to
Friday or collected from
St Margaret's parish
church office at 176
Restalrig Road South
between 9.00am and
5.00pm Monday to
Friday.
Tel: 0131 554 7400.

The story of St Triduana is shrouded in the mists and ambiguity of time, but probably developed to explain a natural phenomenon and as a way of attracting pilgrims and sufferers. Believed to have been born at Colossae, Turkey, in the fourth century, Triduana (Tredwell) was said to have accompanied St Regulus on his flight from Greece to Scotland with St Andrew's relics. For a number of years Triduana led an enclosed life as a nun at Rescobie in Forfar. She was of aristocratic birth, a beautiful and highly virtuous woman. Although a local nobleman, Prince Nectan, wanted to marry Triduana, she had no intention of accepting. She asked the prince's messengers what it was that so appealed to him and they answered that it was the beauty of her eyes. Triduana told the messengers, 'What he admires most in me, he shall have.' She left the room, gouged out her eyes and came back with them impaled on a wooden skewer. 'Take what your prince so much desires,' she said to Nectan's messengers. After this extraordinary self-mutilation to preserve her life as a nun, Triduana is said to have crossed the River Forth and settled at Restalrig, then a village east of Edinburgh, devoting herself to prayer and fasting until her death many years later.

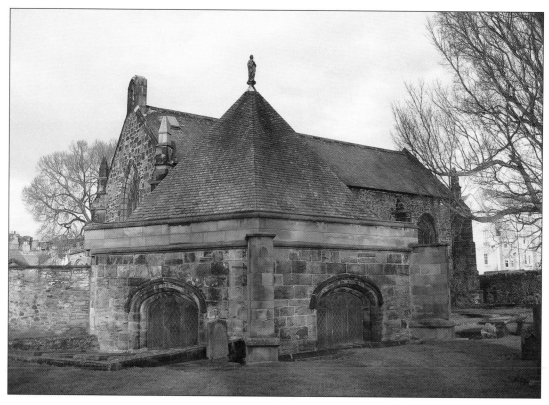

(By permission of Historic Scotland)

Even while Triduana was alive, Restalrig became a place of pilgrimage for those suffering from diseases of the eyes. In 1447 King James III endowed a chaplaincy in the upper part of the parish church of the Holy Trinity and Blessed Virgin of Restalrig – this later became a chapel royal. Ten years later Pope Innocent VIII upgraded the chapel to a collegiate church.

By 1496, when King James IV succeeded his father (who had died at the Battle of Sauchieburn), there were eight prebendaries (canons) under a dean. One canon was in charge of church music, another was the sacristan. Each had a room and a garden and there was a singing-school for choirboys. When James IV was killed at the Battle of Flodden in 1513, the requiem masses sung at Restalrig must have been doubly poignant, for he had been an active and generous patron of the shrine. Within two years James V had completed the foundation at Restalrig (then the parish church of Leith), placing the final coping-stone himself. At the Reformation the General Assembly of the Church of Scotland ordered Restalrig Kirk, as a 'monument of idolatry', to be 'razed and utterly cast down and destroyed'. Today, part of the chapel has been restored.

Prestonfield

Access

South down Dalkeith Road, turning left at Priestfield Road.

A Visit Scotland five-star hotel, awarded the 2005 title of 'Hotel of the Year' from the AA as well as the Room for Romance award, Prestonfield, with its stunning and authentically historic interior, is one of the jewels of Edinburgh tourism. The name Prestonfield was originally 'Priestfield'. From the thirteenth century the property belonged to a Cistercian monastery in Cumberland but since 1376 the lands of Prestonfield have been in secular hands.

The first Prestonfield House may have been a simple fortified tower but in 1681 it was burnt down during a student demonstration and the present mansion was then constructed for its owner, Sir James Dick (1643–1728), Lord Provost of Edinburgh. Designed by Sir William Bruce (who also remodelled Holyroodhouse), the new Prestonfield House was largely completed by 1687. Sir Alexander Dick (1703–85) qualified as a doctor and in 1727 became a Fellow of the Royal College of Physicians, Edinburgh. He succeeded to his father's estate in 1746 and ten years later was elected President of the Royal College.

Sir Alexander entertained many persons of distinction, including the American scientist Dr Benjamin Franklin (1706–90), who visited Prestonfield in 1759 and commemorated his stay in these grateful verses:

> Joys of Prestonfield, adieu!
> Late found, soon lost, but still we'll view
> Th'engaging scene, – oft to these eyes
> Shall the pleasing vision rise.

(By permission of Prestonfield)

> Cheerful meals, balmy rest,
> Beds that never bugs molest,
> Neatness and sweetness all round,
> These – at Prestonfield we found.

Dr Samuel Johnson, the eminent English critic and lexicographer, along with his admiring biographer James Boswell, dined at Prestonfield in November 1773. Their host, Sir Alexander, noted in his diary: 'I gave Mr Johnson rhubarb seeds and some melon.' Eating rhubarb was a daily passion for the fastidious Englishman, who constantly worried about the working of his bowels.

The eminent Scottish judge and historian of manners, Henry, Lord Cockburn (who, as a boy, often played in the grounds of the house), gives this affectionate picture: 'All between the loch and the house was a sort of Dutch garden. It had several long smooth lanes of turf, anciently called bowling-alleys, fountains, carved stone seats, dials, statues and trimmed evergreen hedges. How we used to make the statues spout!'

Today Prestonfield is a world-class hotel with a superior reputation for good food in intimate and tasteful period surroundings. In the grounds brilliant peacocks roam at will, while, close by, eager golfers chase little white balls over the green humps of the *runvig* (medieval ridge and furrow).

Duddingston Loch

Two hundred years ago, when Duddingston Loch became a sheet of glittering ice from the gloomy Hangman's Crag to the garden of Duddingston Manse, it was time for the local curling society to gather. From its foundation in 1795 the society's annual activities began with the Edinburgh magistrates, who 'headed a curling procession to the Loch, returning in the evening in similar order'. The riotous scene has been comically recorded by Charles Doyle (1832–93), the novelist Sir Arthur Conan Doyle's father, in his *Curling Match at Duddingston* and *The Winning Shot at Duddingston*, both in the Edinburgh City Art Collection.

Access

Most easily viewed from the car park in the Queen's Park at the Duddingston entrance.

(By permission of the National Trust for Scotland)

Skating was a hugely popular sport. Professor John Wilson, in his *Noctes Ambrosianae* written in racy Scots dialect, gives a vivid account of the experience of flying over the ice:

> I was at Duddingston Loch on the great day; twa bands o' music gave a martial character to the festivities. I then drew in my mouth, puckered my cheeks, made my een [eyes] look fierce, hung my head on my left shouther [shoulder], put my hat to the one side and so, arms akimbo, off I went in a figure 8, garring the crowd part like clouds and circumnavigatin' the frozen ocean in the space of about two minutes.

The most evocative image of a skater at Duddingston is the graceful painting of *Revd Dr Robert Walker skating on Duddingston Loch* by Sir Henry Raeburn. John Thomson (1778–1840), minister at Duddingston from 1805, was a talented painter who devised a clever strategy for having 'quality time'. He gave a turreted retreat in the manse grounds down by the loch the name 'Edinburgh' and trained his maid to tell visitors that the minister was not available as he was busy in Edinburgh!

The Sheep Heid Inn

Access

Nos 43–5 The Causeway, Duddingston village.

Established in about 1360, the Sheep Heid Inn in Duddingston is thought to be Scotland's oldest public house. The inn was named after a snuff-box made out of the head of a ram. Among the inn's celebrated patrons over the centuries are said to have been Mary, Queen of Scots, her son King James VI and Bonnie Prince Charlie, who slept a night in the village on the way to victory at the Battle of Prestonpans. The inn was once famous for a dish made from the roasted head of a sheep, and in token of his enjoyment of the fare provided King James is believed to have presented the tavern with a ceremonial ram's head. In 1724 the body of Maggie Dickson, hanged in Edinburgh for concealing the birth of a still-born child, was brought to the inn in her coffin on the way to Inveresk for burial. As the burial-party took refreshment at the inn, a noise was heard from the coffin. The lid was prised open and Maggie was found to be still alive. Known henceforth as 'Half-Hangit [hanged]' Maggie, she lived to a ripe old age as an innkeeper and died in the arms of a final lover!

A game of skittles played in the inn's skittle alley was a favourite amusement of patrons, whether workers at the end of a shift or skaters and curlers from nearby Duddingston Loch. In more recent times the former American President Jimmy Carter and his family enjoyed a game in the skittle alley. For a game of skittles book on 0131 656 6951.

Today in the bar, hanging below the ram's head, is a venerable coach licence plate from the days of good King George with the inscription 'G. R. (2 crowns) 255' – a souvenir of the old stagecoach days when the inn was a watering-hole of choice for weary travellers.

Portobello

Access

North of Edinburgh on the shores of the Forth, with long flat beaches.

In the twelfth century what is now Portobello was part of the Royal Forest of Drumsheugh (where King David I liked to hunt). Up to 1750 there was scarcely a house to be seen in the area. The exotic name 'Portobello' was taken from the pantiled (roofed with red Dutch clay tiles) stone dwelling built near what is now Portobello police station. This was the home of George Hamilton, a sailor in the British fleet which captured the Spanish town of Puerto Bello in Panama in November 1739.

The Spanish War ended in 1744 and Hamilton retired from active service to set himself up at the seaside as a cobbler and harness-maker for passing coaches and carriages. He sold food and drink to travellers and serviced the horses, and seems to have especially attracted members of the horse-racing fraternity. By 1753 there were races beside Hamilton's property on the flats of the Freegate Whins, with a silver cup or a saddle for the winner.

In 1763 William Jameson, the son of an Edinburgh builder, won a contract for the construction of the New Town and bought 40 acres of the Figgate estate with its deep bed of clay, with which he began to manufacture building bricks. By 1779 there were three brickworks in the area, with their distinctive beehive-shaped kilns.

A harbour was built in 1788 to service the tile and brick export trade, while a burn was diverted to provide power for other industries, including flax mills, potteries and a soap works.

An industry of a very different kind emerged at Portobello in 1795 when its sheltered beach was provided with the first bathing-machines, so challenging nearby Leith Sands, which until that date had been Edinburgh's only bathing resort. Then two mineral springs were discovered and Portobello became a spa, centred around a basin bubbling with water coloured red by oxide of iron and containing sulphate of lime and magnesia. Portobello Sands also became a favourite place for military drill and even the more disreputable sport of sword-duelling.

As early as 1745 the beach at Portobello had been the setting for the military review conducted by Prince Charles Edward Stuart on 28 October prior to his invasion of England. In the nineteenth century the soldiers at Piershill Barracks, the Mid-lothian Yeomanry Cavalry and the Edin-burgh Light Horse often drilled there.

The novelist Sir Walter Scott, who was over 6 feet tall, was for a time Quarter-master of the Light Horse, and in the intervals between the drills he would walk his powerful black horse up and down the sands on his own, occasionally charging dramatically into the pounding surf with the spray flying all around him. In the drill itself Scott would charge furiously at turnips set on poles, slicing them to pieces with his fearsome-looking sabre as he galloped past.

The military review held at Portobello Sands on 23 August 1822 for the benefit of King George IV is wonderfully recorded in a painting by William Turner (now at the Scottish National Portrait Gallery): the sea is full of yachts, the sand obscured by the smoke of cannon and the general public crammed into carriages or booths which served spirits, porter and ale. It is believed that some fifty thousand people were present.

In later years the fun-loving Prince of Wales (the future Edward VII), a student in Edinburgh under the supervision of the Rector of the Royal High School, came down to Portobello Sands nearly every morning to drill with the 16th Lancers (then quartered at Piershill Barracks). Portobello, with its sands, shows and cafés, has been from time immemorial one of the places where the people of Edinburgh could relax and enjoy a day out.

Portobello – Hugh Miller

Portobello also had a darker side. For four years (1852–6) the geologist and theologian Hugh Miller (1802–56) lived at Shrub Mount, a detached two-storey house with its own grounds constructed in about 1787 off Portobello High Street. Today the front garden is occupied by shops but

Access

Commercial properties and private homes at 80 Portobello High Street.

Miller's house, with its back to the sea, can still be seen behind 80 High Street. Here Miller set up his geological museum, with many of the specimens he had found locally in the Joppa Quarries or in the coal-pits nearby at Niddrie. In Portobello Miller gave lectures on geology and regularly attended services of the Free Church of Scotland.

Miller was born in Cromarty and his early childhood in the countryside taught him a respect for nature and the environment. When he came to Edinburgh he was shocked by its urban squalor. He worked first as a stonemason on Niddrie House in the south of the city but in his free time scoured the volcanic formations of the Queen's Park for rock specimens.

In 1834 he was employed as an accountant with the Commercial Bank in Edinburgh but by 1839 he had become editor of an Evangelical paper, the *Witness*. Over the next few years he was gradually acclaimed as one of the literary giants of Edinburgh. But Miller had a deep-seated persecution complex. He had a nagging fear of being attacked during the night and slept with a loaded revolver, a knife and a sword by his pillow; in his garden at Shrub Mount he installed a powerful man-trap as a protection against burglars.

Then on Christmas Eve 1856 Miller, wracked with horrible premonitions of being assaulted while he slept, put his gun to his chest and shot himself. A note to his wife read: 'Dearest Lydia, my brain burns. I *must have walked*; and a fearful dream rises upon me. I cannot bear the horrible thought.' Miller was widely liked and admired, and when his funeral procession passed through the streets of Portobello south to the Grange Cemetery in Newington there were few onlookers who could hold back their tears.

Portobello – Sir Harry Lauder

Access

A private residence at 3 Bridge Street, off Portobello High Street.

Sir Harry Lauder (1870–1950) was born in a single-storey cottage with a red pantiled roof at 3 Bridge Street, Portobello. His father was a potter who made ceramic bottles for lemonade and jam. Some time after Harry's birth his father went east down the coast to work in a Musselburgh pottery and the family moved to 'the Honest Toun' where, on the golf links, the young Harry later earned pocket-money as a caddie.

After his father died in 1882 Lauder moved north to Arbroath where he found employment as a flax-spinner; later he went west to work as a miner in Lanarkshire. By 1894 he had, however, begun to earn a living in Glagow as a professional entertainer and in 1900 made his debut in London, where he bowled his audiences over. The first of his American tours followed, with Lauder commanding a fee of over $4,500 a week in Times Square, New York.

Sir Harry, with his engaging optimism and down-to-earth common sense, became, along with the Italian operatic tenor Enrico Caruso and the Australian soprano Dame Nellie Melba, one of the biggest record-sellers in the world.

When Sir Winston Churchill was given the Freedom of Edinburgh in the Usher Hall he insisted that Sir Harry sing 'Keep Right on to the End of the Road'. Today the Portobello stretch of the Edinburgh bypass has been named after Sir Harry.

OUTER EDINBURGH (WEST)

Palais de Danse, Fountainbridge

The Fountainbridge Palais de Danse opened in 1920. In those early days it was the resort of the West End set with their shining limousines, white ties and tails, fur wraps and long sheath dresses. Inside, the ballroom was covered in streamers and balloons, with exciting lighting effects. From above the dancers' heads came the choruses played by Jean Morel on tenor sax while perched on the centre of the roof support. Mecca took over the premises in 1938 and it was run by the Delfont Brothers. While still Prince of Wales, the Duke of Windsor visited the Palais with the Duke of Kent, and danced with red-haired Jose Kelly, one of the instructors. In a 'box' or 'pan' at the foot of the main staircase were the instructors (male and female) who could be hired for a dance. Thousands of couples first met at the Palais, and many of the best bands played there: Nat Gonella in the early 1940s, Victor Sylvester in 1944 and Geraldo in 1952. In 1945 the Hollywood film star Sabu the Elephant Boy danced there, while Sarah Vaughan announced in 1953 that she had 'had a ball' at the Palais. In later years the film star Sean Connery worked at the Palais as a bouncer. In 1967 the Palais closed for refurbishment and reopened several years later as a bingo-hall.

Cockburns

Access

Unit 3, Abbeyhill Industrial Estate, Abbey Lane (off London Road and opposite Earlston Place).

Scotland's oldest surviving wine merchant, Cockburns, has a long, distinguished but complicated history. Although Robert Cockburn (Henry, Lord Cockburn's younger brother) started dealing in wine as early as 1796, the Cockburn family had been landowners for over five hundred years. As well as Henry Cockburn, they had produced another eminent legal personality, Sir Alexander Cockburn, Lord Chief Justice of England.

Robert, Henry and their other brother John were sons of the celebrated Laird of Cockpen, Archibald Cockburn. In 1805 they founded R. & J. Cockburn, wine merchants. Nine years later Robert sailed to Oporto in Portugal where he established the firm of Cockburn & Wauchope, which in 1830 became Cockburn & Greig. Robert Cockburn's commercial undertakings included Cockburn & Smithies & Company, Oporto wine-shippers in England, which became a highly respected company.

John broke away from his brothers to set up on his own and in 1831, founded Cockburn, Campbell & Company. The new firm prospered and even received an order in 1832 from the prime minister of the day, Earl Grey, for 22 dozen bottles of claret and 50 dozen of East India sherry. From Sir Robert Peel came a request for 6 dozen bottles of claret.

(By permission of Cockburns)

When George IV was entertained to a banquet in Edinburgh's Parliament Hall in 1822, it was to R. & J. Cockburns that the Town Council sent for their finest wines.

Robert Cockburn's circle of friends and acquaintances included the greatest literary figures in Britain – Sir Walter Scott, for example, who was often to be seen patronising Robert Cockburn's cellar at Sugarhouse Close in the Kirkgate of Leith. During George IV's state visit in 1822 Scott ordered 350 dozen bottles of wine and 36 dozen of spirits. In his *St Ronan's Well*, Scott mentions with relish Cockburns' 'bottle of particular India sherry'. In *The Fortunes of Nigel*, referring to the colour of the wax which sealed their corks, he writes of 'Cockburn's choicest black and blue'. At Cockburns can still be seen the desk used by Sir Walter and Robert Cockburn's high-backed stool, itself also frequently used by Scott.

A letter survives from Scott to Cockburn enquiring 'Will you oblige me by sending with the Melrose carrier to Abbotsford, three dozen of champagne, white and sparkling' – the latter being Scott's favourite tipple, its widespread popularity being due in no small measure to his own influence. Also at Cockburns is a letter dated Hogmanay 1868, written from Kent by the novelist Charles Dickens, who visited Edinburgh frequently. In it he enclosed a crossed cheque payable to order for £35 and 8 shillings, the cost of a cask of whisky. In addition, the firm holds letters from the writer Thomas Carlyle and an enquiry of 1813 from the Duke of Buccleuch, asking about a prize cargo of Dutch gin, newly landed at Leith. Cockburns have recently located to new premises at Abbeyhill.

DISCOVERING EDINBURGH'S PAST

The Central Library

'Who could ever hope to tell its story, or the story of a single wynd in it?' wrote Sir James Barrie, once an impoverished student studying at Edinburgh University. Fortunately, through the generosity of another Scot, Andrew Carnegie, there are resources today which can help to unpick that story. The Carnegie Central Library just off the High Street is an Aladdin's Cave of information. The best way to start researching Edinburgh's history is by reading one of the well-known Edinburgh general histories listed at the back of this book. Visiting a tourist information website in advance is also worthwhile to lay the groundwork for your own personal experience of the city.

When you get to Edinburgh, an overview from the main tourist information centre (TIC) at the east end of Princes Street is a useful and practical way of starting to discover more about Edinburgh's history. At Edinburgh Council's Central Public Library on George IV Bridge (just off the top of the High Street) you will find the information on Edinburgh located in different parts of the building. The Scottish Library, for example, focuses on Scotland in general, while more specialised details of Scottish culture can be found in the Art and Music Libraries; the Reference Library, meanwhile, offers a broad range of knowledge on universal topics.

However, the Edinburgh Room of the Central Library is the unique repository of a wonderfully diverse cornucopia of books, maps, photographs, newspapers and many other official and unofficial records (such as censuses, film or theatre posters) about Edinburgh. Part of an Andrew Carnegie-funded Library, the Edinburgh Room contains the most comprehensive collection in the world of published material relating to the history, topography and social life of the City of Edinburgh (over 100,000 items). Although the Edinburgh Room (like the Reference Library) is not a lending library (unlike the Music, Art, Fiction and Scottish libraries) the material at the disposal of the general public includes colour transparencies (over 6,000), black and white lantern slides, maps and plans, newspapers (from the mid-eighteenth

Access

George IV Bridge (west side).

century), over 300 periodicals, over 11,000 photographs and prints, an extensive collection of press-cuttings, rare and valuable materials and valuation and voters' rolls.

National Library of Scotland

If you can't find what you are looking for at the Central Library, the next step is to cross the road (George IV Bridge) to the imposing National Library of Scotland for further research. You will need to show proof of identity (not necessarily a passport) to obtain a day entry ticket. The National Library contains an enormous depth of primary documents and publications relating to Scotland and is the main Scottish reference library; as a library of legal deposit, it is entitled to claim a copy of all printed works published in the United Kingdom and in the Republic of Ireland. The National Library in 1925 became the successor to the Advocates Library which was founded in 1680 by Sir George Mackenzie (1636–91); among the Keepers of the Advocates Library was the philosopher David Hume, who was thwarted in his ambition to become a professor at the university because of his supposedly atheistical views. The earliest book in the National Library is a copy of the Gutenburg Bible of 1455; also there are the earliest books printed in Scotland – eleven verse pamphlets printed in Edinburgh by Walter Chepman and Andrew Myllar in 1508 – which are part of its collection of 500 fifteenth-century books and 190 of the 400 sixteenth-century recorded works printed in Scotland. Among other books published by Chepman is a copy of the Aberdeen Breviary (Edinburgh, 1510), the only large work by Chepman which survives, and another copy of a first volume of the Breviary brought to Edinburgh from Leningrad at the time of the Russian Revolution. Among the library's special collections are those on bakery and confectionery, phrenology, shorthand, accounting and printing; the Walter B. Blaikie Collection is entirely devoted to Jacobite material. Among the extensive collections of maps at the nearby Map Library at Newington are those made by various Edinburgh engravers and publishers, such as the Lizars and the Bartholomews.

Other Specialist Archives

Nearby on the High Street, deep in the City Chambers, are the City Archives for those seeking information on the history of the city's administration. Finally the Special Collections department at the Edinburgh University Library in George Square (a five-minute walk to the south) contains documents relating to the history of the university and other institutions (such as the history of medicine). General Register House (at the east end of Princes Street) and West Register House (at Charlotte Square just off the west end of Princes Street) house important national documents (such as charters). Births, marriages and deaths are accessible at New Register House. For those interested in Scotland's monuments and architecture, the Royal Commission on the Historic and Ancient Monuments of Scotland (RCHAMS) has a wide collection of information and photographs (including aerial photographs) of Scotland's historic architecture.

The Scottish Catholic Archives holds the largest body of material in the UK relating to the Scottish Catholic Church at home and abroad in the post-Reformation period, as well as parish registers for certain parts of Scotland. The archive holds approximately 250,000 items of correspondence dating from about 1627 to 1900.

Historical Search Room
National Archives of Scotland
HM General Register House
2 Princes Street
EDINBURGH EH1 3YY
Tel: 0131 535 1334
Email: enquiries@nas.gov.uk
Web: www.nas.gov.uk

West Search Room
West Register House
Charlotte Square
EDINBURGH EH2 4DJ
Tel: 0131 535 1413
Email: wsr@nas.gov.uk
Web: www.nas.gov.uk

General Register Office for Scotland (for births, marriages, deaths)
New Register House
3 West Register Street
EDINBURGH EH1 3YT
Tel: 0131 334 0380
Email: records@gro-scotland.gov.uk
Web: www.gro-scotland.gov.uk
Web: www.scotlandspeople.gov.uk (parish register, civil registration, census)

Scottish Genealogy Society Library and Family History Centre
15 Victoria Terrace
EDINBURGH EH1 2JL
Tel: 0131 220 3677
Email: info@scotsgenealogy.com
Web: www.scotsgenealogy.com

Edinburgh City Archives
City Chambers
High Street
EDINBURGH EH1 1YJ
Tel: 0131 529 4616
Web: www.edinburgh.gov.uk

Edinburgh Room
Edinburgh City Libraries
George IV Bridge
EDINBURGH EH1 1EG
Tel: 0131 242 8030
Email: eclis@edinburgh.gov.uk
Web: www.edinburgh.gov.uk/libraries

Royal Commission on the Historic and Ancient Monuments of Scotland (RCHAMS)
John Sinclair House
16 Bernard Terrace
EDINBURGH EH8 9NX
Tel: 0131 662 1456
Email: nmrs@rchams.gov.uk
Web: www.rchams.gov.uk

Scottish Catholic Archives
Columba House
16 Drummond Place
EDINBURGH EH3 6PL
Tel: 0131 556 3661
Email: sca@catholic-heritage.net
Web: www.catholic-heritage.net/sca

OTHER USEFUL CONTACT DETAILS

Travel and Security

VisitScotland (Scottish Tourist Board)
23 Ravelston Terrace
EDINBURGH EH4 3TP
Tel: 0845 22 55 121
Email: info@visitscotland.com
Web: www.visitscotland.com

Edinburgh and Lothians Tourist Board
3 Princes Street
EDINBURGH EH2 2QP
Tel: 0845 22 55 121 (inside UK)
Email: esic@eltb.org
Web: www.edinburgh.org

Tourist Information Tel: 0131 473 3800
Traveline (timetable service for trains,
    ferries and buses but not airlines)
    Tel: 0870 608 2608
Edinburgh Airport Tel: 0870 040 0007

Information Centre
Lothian and Borders Police
188 High Street
EDINBURGH EH1 1QS
Tel: 0131 226 6966
Email: high.street.centre@lbp.pnn.police.uk
Web: www.lbp.police.uk

National Organisations

Palace of Holyroodhouse
EDINBURGH EH8 8DX
Tel: 0131 556 5100
E-mail: holyrood@royalcollection.org.uk
Web: www.royal.gov.uk

The Queen's Gallery
EDINBURGH EH8 8DX
Tel: 0131 556 5100
E-mail: holyrood@royalcollection.org.uk
Web: www.royal.gov.uk

Scottish Parliament
EDINBURGH EH99 1SP
Tel: 0131 348 5000 or (local rate for
    a UK call) 0845 278 1999
Email: sp.info@scottish.parliament.uk
Web: www.scottish.parliament.uk/

Supreme Courts of Scotland
Parliament House
Parliament Square
EDINBURGH EH1 1RG
Tel: 0131 225 2595
Email: Supreme.Courts@scotcourts.gov.uk
Web: www.scotcourts.gov.uk

Historic Scotland
Longmore House
Salisbury Place
EDINBURGH EH9 1SH
Tel: 0131 668 8600
Email: Hs.events@scotland.gsi.gov.uk
Web: www.historic-scotland.gov.uk

The National Trust for Scotland
Wemyss House
28 Charlotte Square
EDINBURGH EH2 4ET
Tel: 0131 243 9300
Email: information@nts.org.uk
Web: www.nts.org.uk

Royal Museum/Museum of Scotland
Chambers Street
EDINBURGH EH1 1JF
Tel: 0131 247 4422
Email: info@nms.ac.uk
Web: www.nms.ac.uk

National Gallery of Scotland
The Mound, Princes Street
Scottish National Portrait Gallery
    1 Queen Street
Scottish National Gallery of Modern Art
    75 Belford Road
Dean Gallery & 73 Belford Road
A free shuttle bus runs between the galleries
Tel: 0131 624 6200
Email: enquiries@nationalgalleries.org
Web: www.natgalscot.ac.uk

Royal Scottish Academy
The Mound
EDINBURGH EH2 2EL
Tel: 0131 225 6671
Web: www.royalscottishacademy.org

Edinburgh World Heritage
5 Charlotte Square
EDINBURGH EH2 4DR
Tel: 0131 220 7720
Email: info@ewht.org.uk
Web: www.heritage.edinburgh.gov.uk

Edinburgh Tours

*The best way to get an overview of Edinburgh
rapidly and effortlessly is through one of the
popular guided city bus tours which can be
boarded at the many designated stops in town.
The following contact details are for Edinburgh
Bus Tours, an umbrella organisation for
Airlink (Edinburgh Airport to City Centre
express shuttle), City Sightseeing, Edinburgh
Tour, MacTours, Majestic Tour and Lothian
Bus Network:*
Edinburgh Bus Tours Tel: 0131 475 0629
Web: www.edinburghtour.com

Follow this with a guided walking tour:
Auld Reekie Tours Tel: 0131 557 4700
Web: www.auldreekietours.co.uk
City of the Dead Haunted Graveyard
    Tours Tel: 0131 225 9044
    Web: www.blackhart.uk.com
Mercat Tours Tel: 0131 225 6591
Web: www.mercattours.com
The Real Mary King's Close
    Tel: 08702 430160
Web: www.realmarykingsclose.com
The Witchery Tours Tel: 0131 225 6745
Web: www.witcherytours.com
The Scottish Literary Tour Company
    Tel: 08001 697410
    Web: www.scot-lit-tour.co.uk

Edinburgh Events

The City of Edinburgh Council
City Chambers
253 High Street
EDINBURGH EH1 1YJ
Tel: 0131 200 2000
Email: eventsplanning@edinburgh.gov.uk
Web: www.edinburgh.gov.uk

City of Edinburgh Museums & Galleries
2 Market Street
EDINBURGH EH1 1DE
Tel: 0131 529 7902/3
Email: cac.admin@edinburgh.gov.uk
Web: www.cacc.org.uk

City Art Centre, 2 Market Street
    Tel: 0131 529 3993
The Writers' Museum, Lawnmarket
    Tel: 0131 529 4091
Museum of Edinburgh, Canongate
    Tel: 0131 529 4143
The People's Story, Canongate
    Tel: 0131 529 4057
Museum of Childhood, High Street
    Tel: 0131 529 529 4142
Brass Rubbing Centre, High Street
    Tel: 0131 556 4364
*Lauriston Castle, Cramond Road South
    Tel: 0131 336 2060
Newhaven Heritage Museum
    Tel: 0131 551 4165
Queensferry Museum, 53 High Street,
    South Queensferry
    Tel: 0131 331 5545
*Nelson Monument, Calton Hill
    Tel: 0131 556 2716
*Scott Monument, East Princes Street
    Gardens
    Tel: 0131 529 4068

*Admission to all the above is free except for
    those marked *

The Edinburgh Military Tattoo Office
32 Market Street
EDINBURGH EH1 1QB
Tel: 08707 555 118
Email: edintattoo@edintattoo.co.uk
Web: www.edintattoo.co.uk

Edinburgh International Festival
Castlehill
EDINBURGH EH1 2NE
Tel: 0131 473 2001
Email: info@eif.co.uk
Web: www.eif.co.uk

Edinburgh Festival Fringe
180 High Street
EDINBURGH EH1 1QS
Tel: 0131 226 0026
Email: admin@edfringe.com
Web: www.edfringe.com

University of Edinburgh
Old Quad
South Bridge
EDINBURGH EH8 9YL
Tel: 0131 650 1000
Email: communications.office@ed.ac.uk
Web: www.ed.ac.uk

Edinburgh University Musical Museums
Reid Concert Hall
Bristo Square
EDINBURGH EH8 9AJ

St Cecilia's Hall
Niddry Street
EDINBURGH EH1 1LJ
Web: www.music.ed.ac.uk/euchmi/

The List
14 High Street
EDINBURGH EH1 1TE
Tel: 0131 550 3050
Email: mail@list.co.uk
Web: www.list.co.uk

Attractions

Edinburgh Old Town Weaving Company
555 Castlehill
EDINBURGH EH1 2ND
Tel: 0131 226 1555
Email: enquiries@geoffreykilts.co.uk
Web: www.geoffreykilts.co.uk

Camera Obscura
549 Castlehill
EDINBURGH EH1 2ND
Tel: 0131 226 3709
Email: info@camera-obscura.co.uk
Web: www.camera-obscura.co.uk

The Scotch Whisky Centre
354 Castlehill
EDINBURGH EH1 2NE
Tel: 0131 220 0441
Email: enquiry@whisky-heritage.co.uk
Web: www.whisky-heritage.co.uk

Royal Yacht Britannia
Ocean Terminal
Leith
EDINBURGH EH6 6JJ
Tel: 0131 555 5566
Email: enquiries@tryb.co.uk
Web: www.royalyachtbritannia.co.uk

Edinburgh Zoo
Murrayfield
EDINBURGH EH12 6TS
Tel: 0131 334 9171
Email: info@rzss.org.uk
Web: www.edinburghzoo.org.uk

Royal Botanic Garden
20A Inverleith Row
EDINBURGH EH3 5LR
Tel: 0131 552 7171
Email: info@rbge.org.uk
Web: www.rbge.org.uk

Pentland Hills Regional Park
Boghall Farm
EDINBURGH EH10 7DX
Tel: 0131 445 3383
Email: ranger@phrangerservic.demon.co.uk
Web: www.pentlandhills.org

Gilmerton Cove
Mercat Tours
12 Niddry Street South
EDINBURGH EH1 1NS
Tel: 0131 557 6464
Email: mercattours.com

Sir Jules Thorne Exhibition of the History
   of Surgery
Royal College of Surgeons
9 Hill Square
EDINBURGH EH8 9DR
Tel: 0131 527 1600
Email: mail@rcsed.ac.uk
Web: www.rcsed.ac.uk

Royal College of Physicians of Edinburgh
9 Queen Street
EDINBURGH EH2 1JQ
Tel: 0131 225 7324
Email: i.milne@rcpe.ac.uk
Web: www.rcpe.ac.uk

Dynamic Earth
Holyrood Road
EDINBURGH EH8 8AS
Tel: 0131 550 7800
Email: enquiries@dynamicearth.co.uk
Web: www.dynamicearth.co.uk

National Library of Scotland
George IV Bridge
EDINBURGH EH1 EW
Tel: 0131 226 4531
Email: enquiries@nls.uk
Web: www.nls.uk

St Giles Cathedral
Royal Mile
EDINBURGH EH1 1RE
Tel: 0131 225 9442
Email: info@stgiles.net
Web: www.stgilescathedral.org

Royal Lyceum Theatre
30B Grindlay Street
EDINBURGH EH3 9AX
Tel: 0131 248 4800
Email: info@lyceum.org.uk
Web: www.lyceum.org

Edinburgh Festival Theatre
13/29 Nicolson Street
EDINBURGH EH8 9FT
Tel: 0131 529 6000
Email: empire@eft.co.uk
Web: www.eft.co.uk

King's Theatre
2 Leven Street
EDINBURGH EH3 9LQ
Tel: 0131 529 6000
Email: empire@eft.co.uk
Web: www.eft.co.uk

Prestonfield
Priestfield Road
EDINBURGH EH16 5UT
Tel: 0131 225 7800
Email: reservations@prestonfield.com
Web: www.prestonfield.com

Beltane Fire Society
Tel: 0131 228 5353

The Vintner's Rooms
The Vaults
Giles Street, Leith
EDINBURGH EH6 6BZ
Tel: 0131 554 6767
Email: enquiries@thevintnersrooms.com
Web: www.thevintnersrooms.com

The Scotch Malt Whisky Society
87 Giles Street, Leith
EDINBURGH EH6 6BZ
Tel: 0131 554 3451
Email: enquiries@smws.com
Web: www.smws.com

The Witchery
Castlehill
Royal Mile
EDINBURGH EH1 2NF
Tel: 0131 225 5613
Email: mail@thewitchery.com
Web: www.thewitchery.com

Hawes Inn
Newhalls Road
South Queensferry
EDINBURGH EH30 9TA
Tel: 0131 331 1990

Cockburns
Unit 3
Abbeyhill Industrial Estate
Abbey Lane
EDINBURGH EH8 8HL
Tel: 0131 661 8100
Email: sales@winelist.co.uk
Web: www.winelist.co.uk

FURTHER READING

Arnot, Hugo, *The History of Edinburgh* (Edinburgh: William Creech, 1779; reprinted West Port Books, 1998)

Cant, Malcolm, *Marchmont in Edinburgh* (Edinburgh: John Donald, c. 1984)

Catford, Edwin Francis, *Edinburgh, the Story of a City* (London: Hutchinson, 1975)

Cockburn, Henry, *Memorials of His Time* (Edinburgh: Adam and Charles Black, 1861)

Daiches, David, *Edinburgh* (London: Hamilton, 1978)

Gifford, John, McWilliam, Colin and Walker, David, *Edinburgh* (Buildings of Scotland series) (Harmondsworth: Penguin, 1984)

Harris, Stuart, *The Place Names of Edinburgh* (Edinburgh: Gordon Wright, 1996)

Massie, Allan, *Edinburgh* (London: Sinclair-Stevenson, 1994)

Mullay, Sandy, *The Edinburgh Encyclopedia* (Edinburgh: Mainstream Publishing, 1996)

Smith, Charles, *Historic South Edinburgh* (Edinburgh: John Donald, c. 2000)